by I. G.
Edmonds

Our Heroes' Heroes

CRITERION
BOOKS

New York

Contents

ACKNOWLEDGEMENTS

The photographs in this book are reproduced through the courtesy of:

WIDE WORLD PHOTOS:
Sir Winston Churchill
Mickey Mantle
E. C. Mantle

SMALL, MAYNARD & CO.
General U. S. Grant

RAND MCNALLY & CO.
Alexander Majors
William F. Cody (Buffalo Bill)

W. A. TOWNSEND & CO.
Admiral Edward Vernon
Lawrence Washington

U. S. AIR FORCE
John F. Kennedy
Jimmie Doolittle

U. S. NAVY
Joseph P. Kennedy, Jr.
Rear Admiral Richard E. Byrd

U. S. SIGNAL CORPS
General Douglas MacArthur
Lt. Gen. Arthur MacArthur

Photographs

Introduction

Heroes Have Heroes Too

As WE READ of the mighty deeds of our own heroes and see them molded in permanent dignity as bronze statues in our parks, it is hard to picture these impressive figures as boys who had been awed by heroes of their own.

Yet, our heroes had their heroes.

A noteworthy example is General George Washington. As a child our first President was headstrong and quick-tempered. George Washington was quite different from the perfect little lad in the fables of Parson Weems, who invented the tale of the hatchet and the cherry tree. It must have surprised those who knew him as a child that his character developed so magnificently that, as an adult, he was considered as nearly perfect as any man America has produced.

Much of the credit for the remarkable change in George Washington as he grew up was due to the guiding hand of his great hero — a man Washington admired from the time he was six years old until the day he died.

Boys and young men select their heroes from many sources. Some choose the famous. Some admire a relative who may or may not be famous. Occasionally, even an enemy has elicited admiration.

Also, there are those who are not wise in their choice of heroes, choosing the wrong men to admire and follow, with sometimes disastrous results.

In picking our heroes, we do not always expect to repeat the same heroic deed. Rarely is it given for a daydreaming boy to surpass the achievements of his chosen hero, although this has happened. In most cases the dream never comes true, but the heroes of our youth play a definite part in developing the kind of man we become.

Thus we owe a debt to our heroes. Beyond that, we owe a debt to the often forgotten heroes who inspired our own heroes.

Who were our heroes' heroes? In all too many cases so little is known of the childhood of great men that we cannot trace these influences. But many of them are known, and here are some of them — our heroes' heroes. . . .

The Hero of George Washington

America's Big Brother

In the year 1781, just after the fall of Yorktown assured the independence of the United States, General Washington attended a victory dinner.

Admiral le Compte de Grasse, who commanded the French fleet that helped the Americans, brought to the dinner two British naval officers whom he had captured and was going to take back to France to be placed in military prison.

Before they sat down to dinner the admiral introduced one of them to Washington.

George Washington

Lawrence Washington

Admiral Edward Vernon

"Captain Robinson," the admiral said, "let me present a man you *may* have heard of lately. General Washington!"

The British prisoner smiled faintly at the admiral's joke that he may not have heard of the most famous man in the Colonies.

"I think every Englishman, including King George, has heard of General Washington," Captain Robinson said. "In fact, I probably have known of the general longer than any one here."

"Oh?" said the admiral. "How is that, Captain?"

"As a lad in England I attended Appleby School. In my form was a young man from the Colonies. His name was Lawrence Washington. We became quite friendly. He told me a lot about Virginia and places with strange names such as Rappahannock."

"Yes," General Washington said slowly, "that was my half brother, Lawrence."

"I remember," Captain Robinson continued, "how excited he was when a letter came from Virginia saying that he had a new brother named George. I remember him telling me that he couldn't wait to go home. He was eager to teach his new brother the best places to fish and to hunt."

"Yes," Washington said gravely. "He taught me those things. But he taught me more important things as well. He taught me to be a man."

Washington seemed unusually quiet and distant. Captain Robinson thought that he had offended the general by speaking of his dead half brother. He changed the subject and the party went in to dinner.

When the evening broke up, Washington walked with

Admiral de Grasse to the carriage that would take the Frenchman back to the dock.

"Admiral," Washington said hesitantly, "there is a matter—"

"But yes, my friend!" de Grasse cried heartily. "After your glorious victory over Lord Cornwallis you could even ask for my flagship and I would give it to you!"

Washington smiled at the admiral's enthusiasm. Then his face turned grave again.

"It is this prisoner, this Captain Robinson. It pains me very much to think of a friend of my brother being in prison. If it would not embarrass you too much, I would be pleased if you could parole him."

"*Mais oui!*" the admiral said quickly. "But yes, General. It shall be done!"

"It may seem strange that I ask this," Washington said. "But Lawrence was more than a brother to me. He was my best friend. He has been dead now for more than thirty years, but he is still very much alive in my heart."

All who have written about George Washington have commented on the general's admiration for his half brother. Most agree that Lawrence was the great hero of Washington's youth. It is known that Washington kept a framed miniature of his brother on the desk at Mount Vernon where he could have before him the face of the man he admired so much. It was still there when Washington died.

Who was this man whom our hero Washington worshiped as *his* hero? Books about George mention Lawrence, but do not tell much about him.

They say only that he was the oldest son of Augustine

Washington by his first wife, Jane Butler. When his mother died, the boy's father took his eleven-year-old son to England where he was put in Appleby School. He was over twenty when he came back to America and met his half brother George for the first time. George was then about six years old.

Lawrence was back home about a year when he left to fight in the strange "War of Jenkins's Ear." He fought under Admiral Edward Vernon, a fiery old seadog who was then the biggest naval hero in England.

After the war was lost, Lawrence came back home. His father, Augustine, died shortly after, and Lawrence became the head of the Washington family. He immediately started battling with his stepmother, Mary Ball Washington, over George. Lawrence felt she wanted to make a sissy of her outdoors-loving son.

Lawrence lost his biggest fight with Mary Ball. He was right, but he lost. Mary Ball was wrong, but she won. Oddly, we in America can be eternally grateful that the wrong person won. Otherwise, George might have been an admiral in the British navy instead of a general in the Revolutionary Army.

Later, George went to the Barbados with Lawrence in a forlorn attempt to nurse his brother back to health.

This is about all George's biographers tell us about Lawrence. It seems a pity to know so little. Surely if George was "Father of His Country," then our heroes' hero, Lawrence, who influenced him so greatly, must be called our country's "Big Brother."

When Lawrence came back to America from school in England forces were already at work to force peace-loving Sir Robert Walpole, the prime minister, into starting a war with Spain.

We can picture Big Brother Lawrence telling seven-year-old George about it:

"He did it! George, he did it! Surely this is the greatest hour in England's history!"

"But what? Who is 'he' and what did he do! Please, Lawrence, tell me!"

"Admiral Vernon!" Lawrence would be almost beside himself with excitement. "I just came from Williamsburg. The news just arrived from London!

"Do you remember how I told you that the Spaniards captured a British merchant captain named Jenkins and cut off his ear for trading with Spanish colonies in South America?"

"You told me how he kept his ear in a jar of alcohol and went around showing it to everyone," George said.

"That's right," Lawrence said. "Some friends took him to Parliament and he showed the ear in the House of Commons so they could see how honest British seaman are treated by the Spanish. That's when Admiral Edward Vernon jumped up and told Parliament that if they would give him just *six ships* he would capture *Porto Bello itself!*"

"Hurrah!" George cried. "Where's Porto Bello?"

Not that it made much difference to the excited boy. If Englishmen were fighting there and Lawrence thought it wonderful, then surely this was history's most glorious battle.

"Porto Bello just happens to be the strongest and richest Spanish city in the New World!" Lawrence replied, his words tumbling over each other in his excitement.

"And do you know what, George?" Lawrence went on. "He *did* it! They gave Admiral Vernon six ships and he sailed right into Porto Bello and captured the place! Word just came to Williamsburg!"

Actually it seemed to seven-year-old George Washington that six ships were a lot, but if Lawrence said it was wonderful, then it just had to be. But the boy considered that at the moment there were more important matters than war with Spain. England would win, of course, just as Sir Francis Drake's ships had defeated the Spanish Armada in the days of Queen Elizabeth.

"You promised to teach me to swim, remember?" he reminded his brother.

Lawrence's mind was on the glory of England defending an Englishman's lost ear. He did not hear George.

"You promised! You know you did!" George declared.

"Oh?" Lawrence said, recalled from the Spanish Main to the river banks of Virginia. "What did I promise?"

"To teach me to swim! You *know* you did!"

"Yes, I remember, and if a man promises something, he must do what he promises regardless of war, storm, or fire. Now *you* promise me that you will always keep your word."

And so George Washington forgot the "War of Jenkins's Ear" in the excitement of being a boy in Virginia with a big brother who treated him like a man.

But he wasn't to forget it for long. Late in 1740, word

came from London for the Colonies to supply 3,600 troops to help Admiral Vernon mount an attack on Cartagena, another Spanish stronghold in what is now the Republic of Columbia. Virginia was to furnish four companies.

There was difficulty in finding common soldiers. Many convicts had to be taken from jail to make up the ranks. It was different with officers. There was keen competition among the young men to get the few positions.

Lawrence, with the help of rich Lord Fairfax, was one who succeeded. George, we are told, was very proud when he first saw his half brother in uniform.

He was not so happy when he found he would not go along.

There are many who believe that it was the sight of Lawrence Washington in uniform that later led George into becoming a soldier himself.

Lawrence did not arrive in Jamaica, British West Indies, until December. As they pulled into the harbor to wait for Admiral Vernon, the sloop *Wolf* sailed past their troopship. The sloop, commanded by a young Virginian named Dandridge, waved good-by. Dandridge had been their guard against Spanish warships on the voyage from Virginia.

It would have surprised both Lawrence and Dandridge had they known that Dandridge's younger sister would marry Lawrence's half brother George, and that the two would live in a great house Lawrence would build and call "Mount Vernon" in honor of the admiral for whom he had fought in the odd War of Jenkins's Ear.

There was a long delay in Jamaica while they waited for

supplies to come from England. It was February 26, 1741, before Admiral Vernon finally anchored his ships off the coast of Cartagena.

Lawrence was disappointed when the fighting was postponed week after week. The military command was divided. Vernon was in command at sea, but the land fighting was to be in charge of the Army's General Wentworth. Cartagena was so located that the ships could not get close enough to bombard the city. It had to be taken by soldiers fighting on land.

There was one happy circumstance that occurred during this period of inactivity. Captain Lawrence Washington was transferred to Admiral Vernon's flagship and placed in command of a company of colonial troops stationed as Marines. And so he came to know and admire the admiral.

The time passed from February to April and still General Wentworth did not attack. Every day Lawrence saw Admiral Vernon stomping the quarterdeck, roaring his rage at the Army's delay.

Lawrence was on the admiral's side. The Colonial soldiers from America were, too, since General Wentworth had enraged them by not permitting them to leave the troopships. Although the British soldiers were camped on the shore, Wentworth said the Americans were a bunch of convicts whom he could not trust.

The situation continued to worsen. Hundreds had fallen ill because of the unhealthy climate. Water was becoming contaminated and the food was rotting.

Finally, on March 19, a young naval captain named Boscawen came to see Lawrence. Boscawen had recently proved his daring in a brilliant fight with West Indies pirates.

"The admiral," Boscawen told Lawrence, "will attempt to shame the general into fighting. I am to take some sailors and marines and storm Barbadera fort myself. Would you like to take your Colonial company and join in the battle?"

"You mean," Lawrence said, "someone is going to trust us 'convict Colonials'?"

Boscawden smiled. "Don't judge Admiral Vernon by General Wentworth," he said. "He has an eye for men. He personally suggested that you go along on the attack."

Lawrence flushed with pleasure to hear that he had been praised by the man he considered his hero.

"Now here are the plans," Boscawen said, unfolding a map. "The entrance to the bay is blocked by Tierra Bomba Island here. The channel on this side, Boca Grande—Big Mouth—has been closed by drifting sand. The only passage into the bay is through Boca Chica, or Little Mouth, on this side of Tierra Bomba. It is protected by Fort Barbadera here on the east cliff overlooking Boca Chica. There are twenty cannon in it. Our job is to capture this fort."

Lawrence was delighted to go along. They left that night in boats and stormed the fortress before dawn. The exact role that Captain Washington played is not known. But we do know that he performed heroically, for Tobias Smollett wrote in his account, "The Expedition Against Cartagena," that Captain Washington was one of those "who attacked the battery with great valour, repulsed the enemy and spiked up the cannon."

Years later, a famous American historian maintained that

Lawrence never left the *Princess Carolina* during the entire war. But this gentleman wrote about two hundred years after the war. Tobias Smollett, on the other hand, was there as a surgeon's mate. Since his account was written years before George Washington became famous, he had no reason to mention Lawrence unless the Virginian did indeed fight with "great valour."

The attacking party returned to the *Princess Carolina,* but it took another two weeks before Vernon could get Wentworth to attack.

Wentworth now had to use the despised Colonial troops, and they were landed on the beach below Cartagena. When orders did not immediately come to attack Quintas, a fortification protecting the advance to the city, the impatient Americans moved without orders. They captured the mountain La Popa.

At this point things looked good despite the fact that many British soldiers were dying of the jungle fevers. But the jubilation was premature.

Wentworth finally gave the order to attack, and they were instructed to move out under darkness, with Spanish traitors to guide them through the jungle to Fort Lazaro which sat atop a seventy-foot hill guarded by high walls. It turned out that the traitors were not so traitorous after all. They led the Redcoats around and around through the night, so that it was daylight before they arrived at the Fort.

It was too late to go back, so the attack was launched with the Americans carrying ladders to scale the wall. Some actually got through the hail of bullets, but the Spaniards had taken advantage of Wentworth's delay to dig deep trenches around the walls, which made the ladders useless, for they were too short.

Many of the Americans dropped the ladders and, "behaving very bravely," grabbed muskets from fallen British soldiers. Others ran for their lives.

It started to rain after sunrise, but the stubborn forces hit twice again before Wentworth realized it was impossible to capture the fort.

Vernon came ashore that night. His language was bluer than the lightning flashes over the battlefield as he accused Wentworth of losing the war by his delays. The general in turn accused the admiral of failing to use the ships to support the attack.

By now there were only 4,000 of the original 12,000 men left who could still fight. The rest were either dead or sick with fevers. There was nothing to do but stop. The fleet returned to Jamaica and the Colonials were sent home. The War of Jenkins's Ear was lost.

Lawrence came back to Virginia and he was made a major in the Virginia militia because of his splendid fighting at Cartagena.

His plans were to go to England and join the British army, but his marriage to George Fairfax's sister stopped that dream. Instead, he built a home at Hunting Creek and named it Mount Vernon for the man who had captured his admiration.

Soon after this, George's father, Augustine Washington, died, and the boy spent a lot of time at Mount Vernon with his big brother Lawrence.

The boy who was to become America's greatest hero

poured out his longings to Lawrence, who reacted sympa-
thetically to George's longing for adventure. It was the way
he himself had felt when he went to fight at Cartagena.

Inspired by Lawrence's tales of Admiral Vernon, George
wanted to go to sea. Lawrence promised to help, and
managed to get a berth on a ship for his younger brother.

But Mary Ball Washington refused to let her dearly beloved son go away, and Lawrence and George Fairfax had
to argue with her for a long time before she consented.

Just before he was due to leave, however, Mrs. Washington
wrote her brother in London and asked his opinion. He
wrote:

"I understand you are advised to send your son, George,
to sea. I think he might better be apprenticed to a tinker;
for a common sailor before the mast has no means of liberty.
They will cut him, staple him and use him like a dog. He
must not be hasty to be rich, but go on patiently."

"Just what I thought!" Mary Ball Washington snapped,
showing the letter to Lawrence. "George will not go!"

Beaten in this, Lawrence turned to other ways to help
George. He suggested surveying, for it would mean adventure in new lands, and there is still in existence a map
George drew just after his sixteenth birthday. At the bottom
he wrote neatly, "A Plan of Major Lawr. Washington's
Turnip Field as Surveyed by Me This 27 Day of February
1747/GW."

While he was learning surveying, Lawrence was also
teaching his brother to curb a ferocious temper. Once George
rode a stubborn horse to death because neither he nor the
horse would give up the fight to break it to saddle. On
another occasion George got into a fist fight with a man who

spoke ill of George Fairfax. Lawrence, who was as even-tempered as Augustine Washington had been, patiently tried to inculcate this virtue in George.

About this time Lawrence became interested in pushing the boundaries of the Colonies to the Mississippi River in order to keep the French from grabbing the land themselves.

Together with George and William Fairfax, he formed the Ohio Company to bring the land under British control. However, his health failed and he went to the Barbados, accompanied by George, in the hope that he would recover. The trip did not help, and he died soon after.

George Washington inherited Mount Vernon. Also he was elected to take Lawrence's place as adjutant of the Virginia Militia. And he helped, a few years later, to carry out another of Lawrence's dreams when he went into Ohio territory as second in command of General Braddock's forces to prevent the French from grabbing the land Lawrence tried to get with the Ohio Company.

Washington's hero worship of Lawrence was based on several factors. He was a beloved elder brother. And he had the qualities George most admired—honesty, courage in battle, friendliness, and an even temper. Washington cultivated these qualities because the man he was using as a model had them.

Today Mount Vernon, that Lawrence built, is a beautiful shrine to George Washington. All who visit Mount Vernon know the story of our first President, but few realize that Mount Vernon is really a monument to *three* men: the hero, George Washington; the hero's hero, Lawrence Washington; and the hero's hero's hero, Admiral Edward Vernon!

The Hero of General Douglas MacArthur

The Boy Adjutant

THE "BATTLE ABOVE THE CLOUDS" was over. The Stars and Stripes now flew from the top of Lookout Mountain. The Southern forces had withdrawn to make a last stand on Missionary Ridge to the east.

The Ridge, five hundred feet high, looked down on the valley where the Tennessee River looped around the city of Chattanooga. The Confederates, led by General Braxton Bragg, fell into long sets of trenches slashed across the Ridge. On top, the big guns of the artillery were swiftly set up.

Confident now that he could not be dislodged, Bragg

General Douglas MacArthur

Lt. Gen. Arthur MacArthur

waited for General U. S. Grant, leading the Union troops, to make the next move.

On the morning of November 25, 1863, Grant sent General Sherman to hit the north end of the rebel line at Tunnel Hill. Sherman was beaten back. Another attempt to turn the Confederate flank went down in defeat.

Then late in the afternoon Grant decided to hit dead center of the southern line. It would be an uphill fight, running across open ground against an enemy who was protected by trenches.

Grant passed word to Generals Baird, Wood, Sheridan, and Johnson to prepare to attack. A cheer ran through the ranks as the men were maneuvered into position.

On Orchard Knob, where Grant had his headquarters, gun crews stood tensely beside their 12-pounder Napoleon howitzers waiting for the signal to fire. It came. The muzzle flashes of the cannon were the signals to move. Bugles blared out the "charge." Blue-clad soldiers fanned out in skirmish lines to start the climb which would be bringing death to so many of them.

In General Sheridan's division one of the units was the 24th Wisconsin Infantry, commanded by Major Carl von Baumbach. At his side when the attack began was the regimental adjutant.

The adjutant was small—too small for the lieutenant's uniform he wore. It hung on him like a sack. His face was boyish, and his curly hair enhanced his youthful appearance. He was a few days short of being eighteen and a half, but he looked more like a lad of sixteen.

He was a strange sight in an outfit famed for the strength and bigness of its soldiers. Moreover, nobody had wanted him in the unit. He was forced on the regiment because his father was a famous judge with political power. The governor of Wisconsin had given him a commission in the 24th Wisconsin Regiment despite the angry objections of both the regimental and the brigade commanders.

At the first company formation he attended, the adjutant could not make himself heard when he called the companies to attention.

An infuriated colonel wrote the governor, pleading for "a man and not a boy for an adjutant."

The governor refused. Possibly he had his eye on the political power of Judge Arthur MacArthur. But this may not be true. He may have recognized the true worth of Arthur MacArthur, Jr.

If he did, he was the only person, other than the boy himself and his father, who saw the making of a military man in the slight youth the regiment contemptuously dubbed their "boy adjutant."

Years later, a man who was in the ranks the day Lieutenant MacArthur made a fool of himself trying to give orders, wrote about it in a magazine:

"Attention, battalion! Prepare to open ranks!"

"The young-rooster-like voice, slim form, pale face, awkward gait and none too well fitting uniform of the boy, afforded amusement to the thousands of young men of the regiment. And as for the colonel and other officers—well, their savage looks would not make nice pictures.

"When the colonel appealed for a 'competent man and not a boy with an unchanged voice,' the Governor sent back word, 'Give him a chance.'"

They had to take him, but his chance to succeed was rated at zero.

Forty years later Lt. Col. J. A. Watrous, who was there, claimed that when the regiment had its first taste of gunfire at the battle of Shelbyville, the "boy adjutant" was the only regimental staff officer the troops saw during the fighting.

"He rode along the line, smiling like a schoolboy at a snowball fight. There was a lull in the contest. The boy rode well to the front to get a look at the enemy. Returning, he hurried along the line and said to the men, with the same cracked voice that so amused them two months before, 'They are coming, boys! Hold your fire until they reach the brow of the hill and then give them a volley.'

"The 'boys' did as the adjutant directed and the Confederates were repulsed. A different kind of talk was heard about the regiment after the battle. Now all praised the squeaky-voiced adjutant."

They would not have been so surprised had they known something of their boy adjutant's background. He came from a line of fighting Scotsmen. It is a family so old that the Scots have a saying, "There is nothing older, unless it be the hills, than MacArthurs and the Devil."

The family fought in all the Scottish wars, in the Crusades, both against and for the English kings, and in the American Revolution.

Early in his life, hearing Abe Lincoln's story during the

great President's first campaign, Arthur MacArthur, Jr., found his personal hero.

There is a legend that he was lying on the hearth, reading a paper his father brought home, when he first heard of Lincoln. It was a campaign biography of the presidential candidate, and young Arthur was struck by the similarity of a picture of Lincoln reading by firelight and his own present position while reading about Lincoln.

From that moment on he followed everything the Illinois rail-splitter did. All through the South there were threats of secession from the Union if Lincoln was elected.

When news of the election reached him, Arthur rushed to his father. "Is the war beginning?" he wanted to know. "If so, I want to go!"

The war did come shortly afterward, and sixteen-year-old Arthur MacArthur, Jr., was ready. There is a story that his father had to hire a guard to keep the boy from running away to join the army. This may or may not be so, but it is true that Judge MacArthur had a long talk with his son and promised that if Arthur would wait one more year he would then use his influence to get him an officer's commission in one of the Wisconsin volunteer regiments.

MacArthur agreed to wait, although he wasn't happy about the delay. He was impatient to fight on the side of his hero, Abe Lincoln. However, they were not wasted months. The boy began reading everything he could get on military strategy, drills, and regulations.

Judge MacArthur arranged for him to get a commission in the regiment which the Milwaukee Chamber of Commerce

was sponsoring. And two weeks after his seventeenth birthday, on June 2, 1862, he became First Lt. Arthur MacArthur,
Jr.

Between that time and his first battle in October 1862, the
"boy adjutant" had a bad time. Yet so strong was his
character that only he knew how bitter and unhappy the
derision of his regiment had made him.

This contempt suddenly changed when they saw him in
battle. At Stone's River — called the Battle of Murfreesboro
in the South — he again distinguished himself.

But it was at Missionary Ridge that he won his greatest
glory. In the other battles he had performed as a good
officer should. But at Missionary Ridge he moved out of the
class of being just an excellent officer into the select company of genuine heroes.

When the command came to charge the Ridge, Lieutenant
MacArthur was in the forefront. Although he dropped back
quickly, this was not from choice. He wasn't strong enough
to keep ahead of the tough Wisconsin troops.

From the two entrenchments, the Southern forces fired as
rapidly as they could reload. From the summit, the cannon
cut loose and their smoke almost obscured the triumphantly
waving flags and pennants.

Cannon balls shattered trees and ripped bloody holes in
the skirmish lines. Bursting shells flung death in a wide
arc. The gray-clad defenders were putting up a wall of lead.

The advancing Union troops did not try to return the fire
with their rifles. It was useless to try to hit a target on the
run. To stop and aim would have been suicide.

They came on, taking advantage of every bit of natural

cover — a shattered tree trunk, a briar patch, the shallow bank of a brook tumbling down the slope.

The advance slowed, and MacArthur again struggled into the lead. He jumped a small brook and turned to shout encouragement to those following him.

Their number was decreasing alarmingly. The dead were scattered down the entire slope. It seemed impossible that the rest would ever gain the summit.

As MacArthur looked back, he saw the color sergeant fall and the flag plunged into the dirt. MacArthur cried out in horror.

The flag was the soul of a regiment. It was its symbol — its rallying point. Many battles have been won because a waving banner seen through the smoke and confusion of a bitter fight gave confidence when courage wavered. In the days when fighting was a more personal thing than it is in this age of missiles and high-altitude bombing, the cry, "Rally 'round the flag, boys!" had real meaning.

The "boy adjutant" whirled, half-tearing his uniform from his body when it caught in a briar thicket. He grabbed up the staff and raised the bullet-punctured banner into the smoke-filled air.

Around him the embattled Wisconsin troops cheered. Somewhere another officer shouted for them to save their breath for the climb ahead. He was unheard in the deafening crash of cannon and rifle.

MacArthur charged ahead. There was no tougher job on the battlefield than carrying the colors. The flag made a splendid target for enemy snipers. The man who carried the banner was begging to be shot.

The Union forces were sweeping across the battlefield on a
two-and-a-half-mile front. They passed through the timber
and fell in droves while Confederate fire cut them down as
they ran across the cleared field separating defender and
attacker.

The Unionists hit the first trenches and clawed their way
over the dirt breastworks. The rebel fire from above
slackened. They could not shoot into the Yankees without
hitting the Confederate troops still in the first-line trenches.

Bayonets flashed in the sun, guns exploded, and then were
clubbed when desperately fighting men did not have time to
reload.

The Federal troops overran the outpost. MacArthur
jammed his flagstaff into the ground to hold it erect, and
grabbed a shovel. Together with his men he worked
frantically to throw up an earthen barrier against the fire of
the gray-clad soldiers above, who had started to shoot again.
The Confederate barricade had been built for protection
against advancing troops. It offered no assistance from shots
from above.

MacArthur grabbed a soldier near him. "We'll be wiped
out if we stay here!" he shouted above the roar of the battlefield. "Pass along the command to advance! We must go on
or die!"

It never occurred to him that there was another alter-
native: to retreat.

There was too much noise for orders to be heard, no
matter how loudly commanders shouted. It would take too
long to try and pass them along from soldier to soldier, if it
could be done at all.

There remained only one thing to do: the men would follow the flag. He leaped out of the trench and charged forward, the Stars and Stripes waving bravely from the staff in his hands.

Along the two-and-a-half-mile front other flags were moving forward as well. The whole army was on the move — to the great surprise of General Grant. He had given orders for them to stop when they took the first entrenchment and regroup for the second attack later.

"Who gave the order to move forward?" the commander in chief demanded.

Everyone denied passing along such an order.

The awful carnage went on, but somehow the determined army overran the second entrenchment and kept clawing their way toward the summit. The frantic rebels ran out of ammunition and rolled rocks down on the advancing attackers.

It had now become a deadly, bloody game. All along the front, each regiment — each man in that regiment still on his feet — was fighting to be the first to hit the top.

MacArthur, physically not as strong as the rest, lost the race, but his heroism was not lost in the confusion of the battle.

Later, in his official report on the heroism of the Wisconsin regiment, the commander, Major Carl von Baumbach, said, "To the adjutant of the regiment I am more than indebted for the aid and efficient services rendered during the engagement."

It was a proud moment for the formerly despised "boy adjutant" when this was written. Later there was to be a stronger accolade bestowed upon him when he was awarded the Congressional Medal of Honor for bravery above and beyond the call of duty.

On June 10, 1865, almost three years to the day from the time of his enlistment, Lieutenant Colonel Arthur Mac-Arthur Jr. — the youngest of that rank in the Army — was mustered out of the service and went home.

His father was now in Washington, D.C., and so MacArthur dutifully took up the study of law in the nation's capital. He stood it for a year, and then for the second time in his life had the unpleasant job of telling his father that he was going to join the Army.

Judge MacArthur was aghast. Promotions were almost impossible in a peacetime army. Men spent a lifetime in the Army and never got higher than major.

But the younger MacArthur refused to listen. He wanted to be a soldier more than anything else in the world. There was nothing the judge could do but give his blessing. His son was twenty years old and a war hero. He was old enough to know his own mind even if he was not yet old enough to vote.

This time the young man was on his own. His father's political friendships could not get his wartime rank restored. Lieutenant Colonel Arthur MacArthur, Jr., returned to the Army as a second lieutenant.

He was quickly promoted to captain, but it took twenty-three years of chasing Indians across the plains before he was a major. While he was stationed at Little Rock, Arkansas, in 1880, his third son, Douglas, was born. Five years before, he had married a Southern girl in New Orleans, Louisiana.

Her four brothers, all former Confederate soldiers, refused to come to the wedding because he was a Northerner.

Captain MacArthur had fought the Sioux Indians on the plains. Later he chased the Apaches in New Mexico and Arizona.

It was an eventful life, full of danger and excitement. Once, during an Indian fight, the arrows were falling all about them. His wife and younger son, Douglas, were in great danger. But he refused to leave the battle line to protect them. Instead he sent a sergeant. Duty was more important than his personal feelings.

But adventurous as his life was, he was far from the great career he had pictured for himself. Once, before he got into the Army, his mother heard him saying, *"General* MacArthur! Doesn't that sound wonderful!"

It looked then as if he would be lucky to make colonel. But as it happened, MacArthur was a man of war. Unknown to him, a new war was brewing. It would again make him a hero and give him the highest rank in the United States Army.

In 1898, Cuba began to battle Spain for freedom. The United States sent the battleship *Maine* to Havana to protect Americans there. In some mysterious manner the ship was blown up. The United States blamed Spain and this started the Spanish-American War.

MacArthur was eager to go to Cuba, but a large volunteer army was being raised to go to the Philippines, where Admiral Dewey had just defeated the Spanish fleet and captured Manila, the capital.

MacArthur was offered the position of brigadier general

in this volunteer force. Since this was not the regular army, the rank would only be temporary, like his Civil War grade of lieutenant colonel.

In the fighting that followed, MacArthur proved himself as able a general as he had been a lieutenant in the Civil War. His brilliance as a commander won him the position of military governor of the Philippines after the war ended.

He served here until William Howard Taft removed him from the job in very much the same way his son, Douglas MacArthur, was fired nearly a half century later by President Truman.

Once more General Arthur MacArthur came back to the States as a hero. His rank was now lieutenant general, the highest grade in the U.S. Army at that time.

The "boy adjutant" had reached the top.

After he and Lieutenant Douglas MacArthur served with the Japanese forces as American observers in the Russo-Japanese War, the general retired in 1909 — almost forty-seven years from the day he failed so miserably when he tried to shout his first order to the 24th Wisconsin Regiment.

On September 5, 1912, he got out of a sickbed to make a speech before a reunion of the 24th Wisconsin Volunteers. Of more than a thousand comrades-in-arms who marched away to war, only four hundred lived to come home. Now the years had cut these survivors down until only ninety old soldiers were left.

The general talked on, recalling story after story of the days when he fought with them for Abraham Lincoln and the Union.

"Little did we know fifty years ago that we should ever be allowed to gather in this way. Little did we think that on that March to Atlanta so many of us would be spared to see Wisconsin again. Your indomitable courage—"

He faltered, staggered, and pulled himself erect.

"Comrades," he said quietly, "I cannot go on."

They helped him to a chair. He bent over and slumped to the floor. A doctor rushed to his side. Gravely he took an American flag from the wall and spread it over the gallant soldier. It was the very flag, according to legend, bullet-ridden and torn, that MacArthur had carried up Missionary Ridge fifty years before.

This was the man General Douglas MacArthur looked up to as his ideal all the days of his life. Like George Washington who kept Lawrence's picture on his desk, Douglas MacArthur kept Arthur MacArthur's picture on his.

After he was removed as supreme commander in chief of the United Nations forces in Japan, Douglas MacArthur appeared before the Congress of the United States. On that occasion he once again paid tribute to his great father.

There is something strange about the heroic life of Douglas MacArthur and his own hero. Their lives followed almost the same track. Both wanted to be soldiers, but both had to wait a year. Both gained their first fame by leading troops into battle. Both won the Congressional Medal of Honor for bravery above and beyond the call of duty. Both were promoted to the highest rank in the Army at the time they served. Both served in the Philippines at a moment of destiny. Both became governor of a conquered country —

Arthur in the Philippines, Douglas in Japan. Both were removed from these offices in a political disagreement—
Arthur by Taft, and Douglas by Truman.

Many boys have been inspired by their personal heroes,
but Douglas MacArthur was the first to duplicate so nearly
the exact feats of the man he loved and admired so greatly.

The Hero of Buffalo Bill

The Man with the Sacred Word

THREE MEN WERE SEATED at a table in a spare office in Independence, Missouri. One was tall, with a beard like a prophet in the Bible. One was quiet and looked like a bookkeeper. One was short, with a fiery temperament.

"This will be the greatest thing in the history of transportation!" the little man cried, punctuating his words by hammering on the table with his fist.

The bearded man looked out the window. As far as he could see there were wagons lined up. Their white canvas covers gleamed in the brilliant sunlight. The lowing of oxen,

Buffalo Bill (William F. Cody)

Alexander Majors

the neighing of horses mingled with the shouts of men and
the ringing of the blacksmith's hammer on iron hoops for
the wagon wheels.

"What you ask," the bearded man said, "will not pay
one-tenth of its expenses, not to speak of the investment
we must put into it. If we do this, it will bankrupt us!"

He paused and waved his hand at the wagon city
stretching out beyond the window. "In two years time we
would have to start selling off our wagons and stock to meet
our debts. We will be ruined."

"But we must!" cried William Russell. "I promised
Senator Gwin that Russell, Majors and Waddell would start
a pony express run to California. I gave him our word!"

He paused and looked shrewdly at Alexander Majors. He
understood his bearded partner very well. He stopped
shouting and said quietly, "Our honor is at stake, Alex. I
gave the Senator our word!"

Henry Waddell looked anxiously at his two partners. He
seemed to realize what was coming, but could do nothing to
stop it. He knew both William Russell and Alexander Majors
too well to try to stop them.

"A man's word is sacred," Majors said heavily. "If you
have given our word to Senator Gwin, then I will not break
that word even though I know it will ruin us. Tell Senator
Gwin that we will start a pony express line across the Rocky
Mountains from Independence, Missouri, to San Francisco,
California, as soon as we can gather horses, way stations,
and men to ride."

Today, only students of Western history remember
Alexander Majors, but the name of a boy who looked upon

Majors as his hero is still world-famous. It is hard to think of the West without thinking of William F. Cody, known as "Buffalo Bill." Cody was the hero of American youth for more than thirty years as he trouped the country and Europe with the greatest of the Wild West Shows.

Many think that because Cody was a showman and had countless westerns written about him that he was not a genuine hero. This is not true. Long before Ned Buntline started writing his Buffalo Bill stories, William F. Cody had established his reputation as a mighty buffalo hunter, a fearless Indian fighter, and as one of the bravest of the Pony Express riders. When he was only fourteen a fellow rider was killed by Indians and Bill Cody rode both his own and the dead man's route.

He traveled 384 miles through hostile Indian country, stopping only long enough to jump from an exhausted mount to a fresh one. Majors called it "the longest and best ridden Pony Express journey ever made."

So it was that Buffalo Bill, William F. Cody, did not wait until he was a man to become a hero. The hero of such a boy must have been an extraordinary character. And he was.

Alexander Majors was a gentle man in a crowd of the roughest, toughest men on earth. Although he was not rough, in his own way he was as tough as any of them.

In an age when men thought it impossible to drive mules, horses, and oxen without cursing them in the most terrible language, Majors would fire any driver who used a harsh word to one of his animals.

When a man went to work for Russell, Majors and

Waddell, Freighters, he was personally given a calf-bound Bible by Alexander Majors and told that he was not to curse the stock and that he must consider his spoken word as something sacred.

And Alex Majors meant what he said. He made this order stick with some of the world's roughest men.

There is a story that men who worked for him used to tell. It can't be true, of course, but it shows how they felt about the boss.

The story goes that a driver for Russell, Majors and Waddell came home to find Indians attacking his house. His wife was dead. His son and daughter were dying. The house was on fire. His stock had been slaughtered. All his money was gone. The story went on to list every possible misfortune that could happen to a man.

Finally, with a dozen Indian arrows in his own body, the poor driver crawled to the telegraph office. He gasped to the clerk:

"Wire Mr. Majors! Tell him what happened to me and ask him if I can *please* just say, 'Doggone it!' this one time?"

Had Alexander Majors just been a goody-goody man he could not have controlled what Buffalo Bill later called "certainly a wild and desperate bunch of men."

The teamsters knew that Majors was as brave as any of them. So they took his calf-bound Bible and obeyed his orders about cursing.

Alex Majors was a child of the Old West. His earliest memory was of a runaway team. He was sitting on the wagon box with his father when the lines snapped. The horses started to run. Ben Majors could not stop them. The covered wagon bounced wildly over the uneven prairie.

"It's going to roll over and kill us all!" Ben shouted. "We have to jump!"

He grabbed his wife and threw her over the side. Alex and his brother followed. Ben jumped himself. His leg buckled and snapped. He sprawled flat.

"Get me a stick!" he bawled to Alex. "I got to get after that team."

The five-year-old boy helped his father fashion a splint. Then, leaning on his son for partial support, Majors went after his horses.

By the time he was old enough to clear his own farm, Alex Majors was a crack shot and had a magical way with animals. He soon quit farming and started a wagon train running from Missouri to Sante Fe, New Mexico. This meant driving eight hundred miles through hostile Indian territory. In some places the trail was so bad he had to rig a block and tackle to get down steep cliffs. Once he drove through a jungle of rattlesnakes. Majors got out in front of the team, striding along snapping off heads of rattlers with his long bull whip to clear the way.

He was known to the drivers as a man without fear. When his team had ten wagons, a party of Indians ran off with thirty-six of his oxen. Alex was not there when it happened. He had gone ahead to search out the evening's campground.

When Alex found out what had happened, he set out alone to get his stock back. He quickly caught up with the Indian thieves, for oxen travel slowly.

There were six in the Indian war party and Alex was
alone. Still he galloped past them without even a glance in
their direction. He circled the oxen, snapping his bull whip
in the air and hazing them around with shouts of "Ho! Ho!"

The cattle turned and began lumbering back along the
trail they had come over. The astonished Indians sat their
ponies and stared at the bold white man.

Perhaps it was this very boldness that kept them from
killing Alexander Majors. They were all in war paint which
signified their eagerness to kill.

Suddenly the Indians spurred their horses and headed
west. Alex thought he was through with them, but before
long they were back with twenty-five more, including their
war chief.

They circled Majors and his oxen. The chief made a sign
and a brave drew his bow with the arrow aimed at Alex's
chest.

Writing about this fifty years later, Majors said, "Of course
there was nothing I could do. I just kept my eyes fastened
on his."

The Indians were surprised at the apparent fearlessness of
the wagon master. As for Alex Majors, he said later he could
feel a place as large as the palm of his hand squeezing into a
painful cramp in the exact spot of his body where the arrow
was aimed.

But somehow he kept himself from showing any fear which
made the Indian chief look at him suspiciously. He could not
believe the white man could be so unconcerned unless help
was close by. He looked at the horizon beyond which the
Major's wagon train was camped.

His uneasy glance was not lost on Majors. Alex helped the chief think re-enforcements were on the way by rising up in his stirrups and looking in the same direction with great satisfaction on his face.

Suddenly the chief started to bargain. He held up ten fingers to show that he would let Alex go for ten of the cattle.

Alex Majors did some quick figuring. All the money he had in the world was tied up in the merchandise on his wagons. If he lost ten oxen, there would not be enough animals left to get his stock to Santa Fe.

"No!" he said explosively.

The chief stared sullenly at him. Alex stood up in the stirrups again and looked at the horizon.

The chief held up five fingers. Alex's eyes cut across to the Indian brave who held the drawn bow with the arrow pointed at the white man's heart. He shook his head in refusal. He would not part with five.

The war chief's face darkened with anger. Majors glared back. The chief again raised five fingers. Majors raised one. For a long moment the Indian did not speak. Then he turned suddenly and shouted to his braves. They kicked their horses in the ribs and drove ahead to cut one of the animals from the group.

In another two minutes they were gone, leaving Alex Majors in undisputed possession of the other thirty-five oxen.

Majors gradually increased his wagons and his business. Soon he went into partnership with William Russell who was not much of a freighter, but who was very good at getting business from the government.

At this time there was a lot of money to be made carrying supplies to the many Indian fighting posts the Army had in the West as well as to the towns.

Finally Henry Waddell was added to the partnership and they rapidly became the biggest freighting concern on the North American continent.

About this time a woman, recently widowed, came to Majors with her young son.

"Mr. Majors," she said, "this is my son Billy. He admires you a powerful lot and would like to work for you."

The boy couldn't have been more than twelve—if that. "He's pretty young to drive teams," Majors said doubtfully.

"He's real strong and real bright," his mother argued. "I wouldn't let him leave home so early if it was to work for anybody but you."

"Well, maybe we can find something," Majors said thoughtfully turning to the boy. "You look pretty husky. We have a lot of ironwork repairing the wagons. Maybe you could help the blacksmiths."

The boy's face fell. He swallowed hard, fighting to keep from showing his disappointment as he saw his dream of flicking a long whip on a wagon train fading.

Alex Majors noted the boy's expression. This did not move him. It was a rare boy who did not long to drive a freighting team out into the wild prairie.

What struck Alex Majors was the way young Billy Cody swallowed his disappointment without a long useless argument. Suddenly he changed his mind.

"How would you like to be a messenger instead?" he asked. "It isn't driving, I know, but there'll be a lot of riding.

You will carry messages between our wagon trains. That means you'll be going everywhere—Santa Fe, Fort Bridger, Salt Lake City—"

"I'll take it!" the delighted boy cried before Majors could name all the places.

Forty years later, Buffalo Bill, then world-famous and a hero himself to thousands of boys, wrote of his admiration for Alexander Majors.

There was much for a boy of the frontier to admire in the strong, tough—yet gentle—man who started out with two oxen and a covered wagon and, with nothing but courage to help him, built a great business.

But much as there is to admire in Alexander Majors' climb to the top, he showed his best side in the way he failed.

The beginning of the end for the great freighting firm of Russell, Majors and Waddell began in 1859 when William Russell promised Senator Gwin of California that the company would start a pony express line across the Rocky Mountains, running from Missouri to California.

"It will bankrupt us," Majors said. "A rider on a horse cannot possibly carry enough mail to pay one-tenth of the expenses of such a line."

"But you don't understand," Russell said impatiently. "We may not make a profit in the beginning, but we'll make a fortune in the end. Let me explain.

"The Southern politicians in Congress were able to force the mail route from the East to California to go through Texas, New Mexico and Arizona. Senator Gwin feels that this takes too long. He wants an overland mail route—right straight through!"

"The Butterfield stage line was routed through the South to avoid the snow and the roadless mountains," Alex said. "No stage could get over the Rockies."

"Certainly not!" Russell exclaimed. "But a horse and rider can. Congress will not put up money for a mail route by the Overland way because the Southerners, to get the business, have convinced them that a mail route across the Rockies is impossible."

"I agree with them," Waddell said.

"Well, I promised Senator Gwin that we would put in a pony express to prove that it is possible," Russell said. "He in turn promised me that Congress would provide extra money as soon as we can prove that mail can be carried across the Rockies."

"We'd lose thousands," Waddell said.

"No, *hundreds* of thousands," Majors said.

"Gentlemen!" Russell cried. "You've got to stand by me in this matter. I *promised* Senator Gwin. We may lose a little in the beginning, but we'll get it all back and a handsome profit."

"It will bankrupt us," Majors said.

"Gentlemen," Russell said, his voice, usually loud, dropped almost to a whisper as he gave a shrewd glance at his stubborn partner, "Gentlemen, I gave Senator Gwin our word. Are you going to go back on our sacred word?"

Alexander Majors' face looked pained. He did not want to go into a losing business, but as Russell had shrewdly foreseen, he could not refuse. All his life he had preached that a man's word is sacred. He had always demanded of his drivers that each man stand up to his spoken word.

Now that Russell claimed he had pledged the company's word to the California Senator, Alex felt that he could not go back on that word and still retain his self respect. He agreed to go ahead, knowing he would lose everything he had accumulated in thirty years of hard work.

So began the Pony Express—a glorious chapter in the winning of the West. The actual riding of the Pony Express was a boy's job. Strong, fast-riding teen-agers were preferred because their lighter weight enabled them to outrace Indians, plow through mountain-like snowdrifts, take the desert heat, and fight off bandits.

Once, Buffalo Bill was held up. Risking the brandished gun, fifteen-year-old Billy Cody spurred his horse against the bandit's mount and spoiled his aim. This also gave him time to draw his own gun and he managed to get away.

While the Pony Express rider became the new American hero, behind the scenes Alex Majors was seeing his prophecy of bankruptcy come true. It cost the company a hundred dollars for each ten dollars that came in.

Despite the financial drain, Majors was proud of his riders' courage. The high point was reached when they carried President Lincoln's inaugural address across the nation in seven days and seventeen hours.

Majors proudly wrote, "I think, taking the distance into consideration, that this was the quickest time on record in this or any other country."

The route ran from St. Joseph, Missouri, to Sacramento, California, a distance of 1,960 miles. The shortest time made by the Butterfield coaches was twenty-one days on their long detour through the southern section of the country.

Russell was popping with pride at this proof of the value of the Pony Express. But success had come too late. Congress failed to appropriate the money needed to keep the line going.

Both Senator Gwin and William Russell had been sincere in their belief that a subsidy would be approved by Congress. What they failed to foresee was the success of the telegraph. These "strings of steel" were pushed across the country very rapidly when the Civil War made communication with the West Coast so important.

At the end of eighteen months there was no longer need for the gallant pony riders. Majors, Russell and Waddell, were now so heavily in debt that they lost control of their giant freighting firm to Ben Holladay, the stagecoach king.

All Alex Majors had left were a few wagons and some oxen. He started all over again as a private contractor working with his son, Ben, to haul freight to the Union Pacific railroad. As soon as this line connected with the Central Pacific to form a transcontinental railroad, Majors saw the end of the ox-drawn wagon team which had been his life since he left the farm.

He spent the rest of his life in the mining industry, but never again acquired wealth.

If he regretted losing a $2,000,000 business because he would not break his word, no man ever heard Alexander Majors say so.

The Hero of Sir Winston Churchill

The Road to Blenheim

THE COURIER LEAPED from his spent, lathered horse. The Earl of Marlborough did not wait for his aide to open the dispatch case. He scandalized the assembled noblemen by reaching for it impatiently and opening it himself. They thought such a menial task beneath the dignity of an English lord.

But Marlborough was not concerned with their thoughts. He was certain that an important battle—perhaps even the entire war with Louis XIV of France — depended upon the message in the dispatch case.

Sir Winston Churchill

The Duke of Marlborough

He removed the document. As he read it, a pleased smile spread across his pink, handsome face.

"Gentlemen!" he cried. "This is wonderful news. In crossing the Meuse River as we did, we have frightened the French troops into pulling back into Belgium. The threat to Holland is relieved. This dispatch confirms their retreat!"

The group hailed the news with great joy. One of the foreign generals said with great relief, "This means we will avoid the pitched battle which I was certain you would force on us."

"No! No!" Marlborough cried, his flashing eyes turning from first one of the allies to the other. "This gives us a wonderful opportunity to fight and perhaps utterly destroy the French forces here in the Spanish Netherlands!"

The other generals who made up the allied command of what history calls The Grand Alliance of the War of the Spanish Succession were aghast at the idea of fighting the French. Louis XIV had the strongest army in the world. It was suicide for the allies — England, Holland, and Austria — to attack so mighty a force. No, they insisted, the allied forces must be kept on maneuvers and only fight defensively. To take the offensive and attack was unthinkable.

"But look," Marlborough argued. He stooped and traced a line with his forefinger in the dirt. "This is the French line pulling back because their commander mistakenly believes we intend to shift over here."

He paused and drew another line like an arrow. It ran to the center of the line representing the maneuvering French.

"This is our combined forces," he said, his pink face flushing with eagerness. Exposure to sun and wind had not darkened his fair skin as it had that of his companions. "We will hurl them right through the French lines," Marlborough continued. "We will split them in two and then spread on each flank to destroy all the columns!"

"But no one can do that to Louis' army!" another officer cried.

"I agree," spoke up a tall man dressed in civilian clothes.

"And I," said another, similarly dressed. "This plan is unthinkable, my Lord Marlborough. I must exercise my authority and veto so mad a plan."

The other civilian nodded vigorously in agreement. Marlborough slowly rose to his feet. Outwardly his good nature was preserved, but inwardly he felt defeated.

"Perhaps you are right," he said. Years of living in the British court had taught him to hide his disappointment under a cheerful mask.

Actually he saw victory slipping away because of the timidity of his allies. And there was nothing he could do about it. This was a crucial moment in the War of the Spanish Succession which gripped Europe in 1702. They were fighting to keep France from swallowing Spain and after that all Europe.

The planning for the war was done by William of Orange, who had become William III of England. The king intended to lead the armies himself, with Marlborough as his second in command. But William died, and the Dutch, respecting his wishes, made Marlborough commander in chief of the allied forces.

While they did him this honor, they also showed their distrust of his bold ways. They insisted on having two

civilian deputies assigned to the high command. These men
had the power to veto any plan for offensive action made
by the Earl of Marlborough. They exercised this right on
every battle that involved an attack. They insisted that the
army be used for defense only.

This was considered the correct way to wage war in the
late seventeenth century. But the earl—he did not become
a duke until later—had new ideas which were to make him
the greatest military commander of his time. He wanted to
strike boldly, for he saw clearly that without this boldness
the French would win.

That night, in Marlborough's tent, an English colonel
bitterly assailed their timid allies.

"My Lord," he said, "we might as well return to London.
There is nothing we can do here but lose and lose and lose!"

Marlborough smiled as if he had some secret knowledge
that appealed to him.

"No," he said softly, "there is a way. You noticed today
how we fooled the French by pretending to do something
we had no intention of doing?"

"Yes, my Lord," the colonel said. "They were fooled because you pretended to do what military science said was
correct and then did not do it."

"And because we did not follow the textbook," Marlborough added, "the enemy was confused. At that moment
we could have destroyed them."

"I fear it will never be different," the colonel said sadly.

"I don't know," the earl replied with a quiet smile. "It
seems to me that we must do the same thing with our allies

that we do with our enemies. We must make them think we are following the old rules of war while we make new rules of our own. Yes, we must fool both our friends and our enemies!"

"How can we do that, my Lord?" the colonel asked.

Marlborough stuck his finger on a map spread across the table between them. "We will do it by jabbing here—"

His fist clenched and he struck the map a hard blow in another more remote section of Europe.

"—and then striking here with all our force!" he finished.

This was Marlborough on the road to Blenheim. Blenheim was a small village on the Danube River. At that moment it was possible that Marlborough had never heard of the place. It is certain that no one in England had. But soon it would be a name that rang in glory all through the kingdom.

Blenheim changed world history in the seventeenth century as well as in modern times. This came about because the greatest leader of the twentieth century had the Duke of Marlborough for *his* hero.

This hero worshiper was Winston Churchill, Prime Minister of England during World War II—and one of the truly great men in history. Churchill was more than just a great leader. He was also a genuine hero on the battlefield.

As a child, Winston was so dull that his father, Randolph Churchill, despaired of his stubborn son's ever achieving anything. Winston's teachers agreed. What good could come of a boy who, when his schoolmaster said, "I have reason to be gravely displeased with you," replied, "And I have grave reason to be displeased with you, sir!"

About the only thing young Winston seemed good for
was maneuvering his toy soldiers about the room where his
famous ancestor, the Duke of Marlborough, once walked.

This room was in Blenheim Palace where Winston was
born. It had been named for Marlborough's great victory
and had been the Duke's home until his death. The shadow
of the great man was thus constantly over young Winston
as he played at soldiering and dreamed of someday fighting
battles for England as gloriously as Marlborough had.

There is no doubt that Winston Churchill, even as a child,
felt that he was destined to walk in Marlborough's footsteps.
Once, when a larger boy gave him a beating, Churchill,
wild with anger, shook his fist at the victor.

"But I'll be *greater* than you!" he cried.

The other boy, irritated by the youngster's fantastic ego,
proceeded to whack him a couple of more times to teach him
manners.

As his stubborn son grew into his teens, Lord Randolph
decided that perhaps the Army could do something with
him. After three failures, Winston managed to get into
Sandhurst, the British military academy.

After graduation he plunged into war with the same
enthusiasm once shown by the famous Duke of Marlborough.
He fought heroically in Egypt and then in the South African
Boer War. He became a national hero when he engineered
a daring and dramatic escape from the Boers.

Although Winston returned to England and entered
politics, he still looked up to the Duke of Marlborough as
his great hero. As a middle-aged politician, he took time out

to return to Blenheim Palace. His research into old letters and documents led to the writing of a three-volume history of his hero. Even later in life, as a world-famous figure, he was fond of punctuating his speeches with references to "the great Marlborough."

There were those who claimed peevishly that Sir Winston saw himself as a reincarnation of the Duke of Marlborough. While they were alike in many ways, they were very different in others. Marlborough was a handsome man. Sir Winston looked like a bulldog during his mature years. Marlborough never raised his voice. He was quiet, considerate, and diplomatic, whereas Sir Winston was famous for his sharp tongue.

Once, an angry member of Parliament—a woman—told him, "If I were your wife, I'd put poison in your tea!"

He replied in typical Churchill fashion, "Madam, if I were your husband, I'd gladly drink the poison!"

Such a retort would have been unthinkable to Marlborough.

But where it counted, the two men were alike. Both distinguished themselves brilliantly by their resourcefulness and courage during periods of crisis.

In the first bitter days of World War II, after England had suffered nearly disastrous defeats from Hitler's troops, Sir Winston made his famous speech:

"We shall fight on the beaches . . . we shall fight in the streets, we shall fight in the hills; we shall never surrender."

He was simply echoing the indomitable spirit of Marlborough as that great Englishman had once hurtled down a road of defeats to the glory of Blenheim. The troubles of both these heroes were caused by timid politicians who delayed fighting until it was almost too late.

John Churchill, who became the Duke of Marlborough, was sixteen years old on that fateful day in 1666 when he became a page to James, Duke of York and brother of Charles II.

This was a time of great religious strife and almost constant war. As the years passed, Marlborough proved to be one of the country's most brilliant soldiers. He rapidly advanced to colonel, but before he could achieve any further promotion, he was sent into exile.

The trouble was that Charles II was a Protestant king of a Protestant England while his brother James was a devout Catholic. The distrustful British forced James into a three-year exile. Marlborough, although a Protestant himself, chose to share the Duke's exile.

Three years later, Charles forced Parliament to permit his brother to return to England. Marlborough came back with him. When Charles died, Protestant England found itself with a Catholic king. Immediately the Duke of Monmouth, James's half brother, invaded England to "bring back to the people a Protestant king."

Marlborough's father, the first Sir Winston Churchill, learned of Monmouth's landing and rushed to London to sound the warning. Marlborough was sent with troops to destroy the invader, but before the two armies met, King James sent his favorite, the Earl of Feversham, to command the army.

Marlborough was bitter at being dropped to second in command. He wrote in a letter to his wife, "It seems that I must do the work and let another have the honor."

And it was to be just as he thought. Monmouth made a surprise attack in the night. Lord Feversham was overwhelmed with confusion and Marlborough had to rally the British troops. He struck the enemy so fiercely that their ranks broke. Monmouth, seeing that he had lost, deserted his troops. Later he was found cowering in the bushes. He was dragged to London and executed.

Marlborough came back to London to find that Lord Feversham had indeed received all the credit for the victory. This was discouraging. Perhaps it was this unfair treatment that caused him to join those who supported the Dutchman, William of Orange, in overthrowing James.

Unlike the others who secretly deserted to join the invaders, Marlborough wrote James a letter. He told the king that his decision to support William was based on his religious beliefs.

After the Revolution of 1688 put William and Mary on the throne of England, Marlborough became important once more. He put down the revolt in Ireland and helped defeat Louis XIV of France when that warlike king tried to restore James to the English throne.

Two years later, William started to plot another war with France. The excuse came when King Charles of Spain died childless in 1700. His will left the throne to Philip of Anjou, grandson of Louis XIV.

All Europe shivered. The combined might of France

and Spain might enable Louis to conquer all of Europe, as
he had been trying for years. William immediately sent
Marlborough to form a second Grand Alliance, banding
together the enemies of Louis XIV for a new war.

This Marlborough did with such success that he was
hailed as a diplomat as well as a great soldier. At this point
William considered Marlborough the second best commander in the world. William considered himself the best.
He said he would lead the armies as commander in chief
with Marlborough as his second in command.

Once again it seemed that Marlborough would do the
work in battle for which another would receive the credit.
However, William died before he could begin the War of
the Spanish Succession. The Dutch, as we have seen, chose
Marlborough to carry on as commander in chief, but with
two civilians to see that he did not fight as he wanted to
fight.

In spite of his difficulties, Marlborough managed to
capture four important French forts and expelled the French
from Holland. He returned to England where the happy
queen made him a duke.

In those days, wars were fought in good weather. During
winter the army went into camps and the commanders
returned home. Anne had made Marlborough her first
minister and he was virtually the uncrowned king of
England.

The second year of the war found Marlborough even more
hampered by his timid allies. The third campaign opened
with a dangerous situation. The forces of Louis XIV were
threatening to overrun Austria, but the Dutch flatly refused

to permit their troops to be drawn away from the Lowlands in order to aid the struggle in Central Europe.

It was at this point that Marlborough decided he had to fool his allies as well as his enemies. They permitted him to take the allied army to the Moselle in Germany, but here he suddenly pulled the British troops away from the Dutch army and started a mad march across Europe.

No one but himself knew where he was going. The allies screamed for him to stop. Marlborough ignored them and kept going. The two civilian watchdogs were left behind. Villeroi, the French general, as puzzled as everyone else, started after Marlborough. The Dutch were now afraid to remain behind and took up the march behind the French pursuers of the great Englishman.

Marlborough did not stop until he reached the Danube River and he was in a position to halt the French advance on Vienna. He had moved 50,000 men over 250 miles in five weeks. For that period this was practically flying.

Once in Austria, Marlborough found himself in the same old trouble. The allied commander there was the Elector of Baden. This stubborn old warrior had different ideas from Marlborough. Moreover, he felt that because he was a prince he outranked a mere duke.

The question of who would give orders was settled in comic-opera fashion. They agreed that they would take turns—one would give orders one day and the other the next.

They finally agreed to attack the enemy at Schellenberg fort. It was Marlborough's day to command. He started moving troops. The Elector thought they would not be in

position to fight until morning when he would take over and
rescind the order. He forgot that the Earl of Marlborough
was a master at moving an army rapidly.

At four o'clock of the same day, while the Elector thought
the battle was still twelve hours away, Marlborough was
already in position and fighting! The Elector was as surprised as the French enemy.

This brought the two armies together for the greatest
battle of the war. Marlborough's previous victories had
been minor affairs. This one was different. For the first time
it was proven that the army of Louis XIV could be met in
pitched battle and defeated.

The French had 20,000 troops dug in about the village of
Blenheim on the Danube with reinforcements on the way.
They were protected on one side by marshes. Rocky wood-
lands and five streams protected them on other flanks. Only
a madman would dare attack so well placed an enemy
thought both friend and foe.

Tallard, the French commander, waited in Blenheim and
prayed that the Englishman would be fool enough to attack.
And attack Marlborough did. His forces came at the French
from three directions, advancing through heavy fighting to
the village outskirts. Here each division waited until all the
others were in position. The French were squeezed so
tightly in Blenheim that they could not maneuver.

Then Marlborough gave the command to charge. A cannon
ball narrowly missed his head. He waved his frightened
aides back, but he gave no more thought to his personal
danger than he had earlier when his horse was shot from

under him. The Earl of Marlborough did not command from the rear. He went into battle with his troops.

When the fighting ended, there were 14,000 French prisoners in his hands. General Villeroi, who had followed the swift flight of Marlborough from Holland, now started to retreat. He had no stomach for fighting just then.

Blenheim made Marlborough one of the great names in British military history, but it did not win the war. The war was never won. Marlborough kept winning on the battlefield until he got so close to Paris that Louis XIV was ready to flee.

However, politics defeated the great general who could not be whipped on the battlefield. Marlborough's enemies at home got him removed as commander and succeeded in ending the war in time to save France from total defeat.

Marlborough was retired from the army and he traveled in Europe until George of Hanover became king when Queen Anne died. The first official paper King George signed was a commission restoring Marlborough as commander in chief of the army.

There were no more wars for him to fight, and he died in 1722. At that time one of his bitterest personal enemies, Lord Bolingbroke said, "He was so great a man that I forget his faults."

The Hero of Admiral Richard E. Byrd

Peary of the Pole

THE STORY OF RICHARD EVELYN BYRD is the story of
courage and a stubborn refusal to quit, regardless of difficulties. An injury ended his active career as a naval officer.
The doctors said he was no longer able to serve, but Byrd
refused to quit. Before his life had run its natural course, he
had become an admiral and the greatest American explorer
of modern times.

Not the least of his accomplishments was his outstanding
ability as a leader. He began polar exploration in the 1920's

Rear Admiral Richard E. Byrd

Robert E. Peary

when equipment was far short of the perfection it is today, but so great was his leadership and his ability to plan his explorations that in more than thirty years of Arctic and Antarctic expeditions he never lost a crew member.

During the long nights of the Antarctic, Byrd often spoke of the great men who had preceded him in the struggles to reach the two poles. When he was a boy and later when he was a young man, it was the dramatic tales of these early heroic explorers who awakened his own burning desire to go first to the North Pole and then to the South Pole. Those who served with Byrd at the Pole have told how he spoke of Lieutenant Wilkes, the U.S. Navy hero, whose heroic journey in a wooden ship proved that there was a continent at the South Pole. He spoke also of Amundsen, the great Norse explorer; Franklin, the British officer who vanished into the Arctic with his crew and ships and never was heard from again. And most of all he spoke of Robert E. Peary, who finally did what Byrd and all the others wanted so desperately to do — be the first man to reach the North Pole.

Many men cannot tell when they first became conscious of a driving ambition. Often the dream which spurs a man on to greatness develops so gradually that the spark which started it is forgotten.

This was not true in the case of Robert E. Peary. His dream began with a book about Greenland which he bought in a secondhand bookstore in Washington, D.C., probably in 1876.

In those days very little was known of this strange ice-locked land. Leif Ericson, the Viking discoverer, gave it the most inappropriate name of Green Land. As the centuries passed, very little more was learned about the area. It was not even known if Greenland was an island or part of a great Arctic continent.

These unanswered questions about the top of the world interested Peary. A few years later he was stumbling through jungle swamps of Nicaragua as a member of a U.S. Navy civil engineering team. Snakes, mosquitoes, rain, treacherous mud, and poor food made it a miserable assignment.

It is little wonder that his mind kept going back to the mysteries of Greenland, that land of everlasting snow and cold. Sometimes he would talk about the place to Matt Henson, his Negro servant. No one had ever been through the entire length of Greenland. They knew that inland there was a great ice plain, but no one knew how far it extended.

"Someday," he told Henson, "I'm going to find out!"

"You must take me with you, Mr. Peary," Henson said eagerly.

"That I'll do, Matt," the young lieutenant said. "Someday —well, maybe you and I will stand on the North Pole itself!"

No dream seemed more unlikely. Some of the greatest explorers in history had failed, many of them losing their lives in the attempt to find the Pole.

Martin Frobisher, Henry Hudson, Sir John Franklin, and others who followed their pioneering efforts to find the Northwest Passage, pushed deeper and deeper into the frozen North. Many of these expeditions had ended in tragedy.

But danger and the risk of failure meant nothing to Peary. The call of the North hammered in his ears as he swung a machete to cut his way through the jungles of Nicaragua.

The call became so strong that, in January 1886, he applied for leave from the Navy. Since the canal survey on which he was working was temporarily shut down he had no trouble getting away. He borrowed $500 from his mother, and without experience or advice set out for Greenland.

All he knew about Arctic exploring was what he had read in books. He paid the captain of a whaler to take him most of the way. The ship dropped him at a small island where he hired Eskimos to paddle him on to the Greenland mainland in kyaks, boats made of skin. On the mainland he engaged an Eskimo guide and they set out in two sleds to climb the ice cap.

What seemed like a smooth plain of ice turned out to be a death trap. Cracks marred its surfaces. In many places packed snow hid the crevasses. The two men slowly climbed nearly two thousand feet upward along the sea of ice.

As he progressed, Peary became more confident— and almost lost his life. He started across a snow bridge that spanned a great fissure in the ice. He took only a few steps when the packed snow gave way.

He felt himself falling. He whirled about, seeking desperately to get back, but he was too late. The snow bridge was crumbling into the chasm. The bottom was so far below, the unfortunate man could not see where it dropped through the solid ice.

He threw himself forward. His hands caught the sharp ice of the crevasse. The ice cut through his mittens. But he was struggling so hard to hold on that he hardly noticed the pain.

His companion grabbed his wrists. He couldn't brace himself enough to pull Peary up. For a moment it appeared that nothing could save the man who had rashly exchanged the jungle for the ice world.

Then Peary managed to get his foot braced against a giant icicle. This eliminated some of the drag on his body. Together the two men were able to work Peary's way out of the crack.

This should have cured him of his unreasonable desire to explore Greenland, but it only whetted his ambition. He looked upon each difficulty, danger, and near escape as another learned lesson. He was studying to be an Arctic explorer in the harshest of all possible schools — on the frozen ice itself.

The great sea of ice kept sweeping upward. Peary was now more than a mile and a half above sea level. The wind whipped and cut constantly, at times with such violence that they could not walk against it.

One day the normally strong wind built into a gale. The dry snow blew and drifted like Sahara sand. It was impossible to move. The dogs crouched in their traces, whining, rolling into balls with their bushy tales pulled around their noses to protect them from the stinging blast of the gale-driven snow.

Peary and his guide flopped on the ice, pulling blankets over them as some protection from the fury of the wind.

Twenty-four slow hours dragged past, but the wind continued to howl and tear across the ice pack.

Of course they could not eat. Even breathing was difficult. Peary's body was cramped. Twice his nose froze and had to be thawed by warming it with his hand.

The storm went on for yet another night and day before it blew itself out. Then the battered men and dogs dug themselves out of the layer of snow that had drifted over them.

The sun came out bringing a blinding glitter to the eternal flatland of ice. Their food was almost gone. The dogs' feet were in bad condition from cuts on the rough ice. Both men were also in bad shape.

After an agonizing struggle with himself, Peary realized that he had to turn back. His dream of being the first man to cross Greenland would have to be realized at some future time.

Before he started back, Peary took a shot of the sun to mark their position. According to his observations, he had penetrated into the interior farther than any man had gone before.

This was some satisfaction and gave him hope for the future. Although he had gone farther inland, other explorers had gone farther north. Robert Peary was still a long way behind in the race for the Pole.

Back in the United States Peary was again sent to Nicaragua on the canal project. Just after it was completed and he was making plans to go north, he got word that Fridtjof Nansen had beaten him to the punch and made the first crossing of Greenland.

In later years Peary's favorite expression was, "If there

isn't a way, I'll make one!" It was the same thing now. Beaten to one goal, he immediately set himself another and more difficult one. This time it was to push on along the ice pack to the top of the world if necessary, to see if Greenland was an island or a great continent that extended all the way to the North Pole.

By 1891, Peary had raised $10,000, and on June 6 he set out for Greenland again in an Arctic whale ship *Kite*. Aboard were Peary's wife (the first white woman to winter in the Arctic) and a doctor named Frederick A. Cook.

In the years to come Dr. Cook was to play the leading role in the bitterest act of Peary's heroic life. Although the two men were to become enemies, Cook was a great help on this second Peary expedition.

As the *Kite* churned through Melville Bay on its way to Inglefield Gulf where expedition headquarters would be established, it hit large fields of ice.

It was well into summer and the ice pack was rotten. For a few days the iron-sheathed nose of the *Kite* sliced through the huge "pans" of ice as the whaler worked its way north.

Gradually the ice floes became harder. Often the ship had to back up and charge several times before it could crash its way through.

Mrs. Peary's journal tells us how it was: "The floe would be shivered just as a sheet of glass is shivered when struck a sharp, hard blow. The pieces were hurled against and on top of other pieces, crashing and splashing about until it seemed as though the water was boiling. But the good old *Kite* pushed them aside, leaving them in the distance groaning and creaking at having been disturbed."

On the afternoon of July 15 a lookout in the crow's nest

reported that he could see clear water ahead. The spirits of everyone went up. They had been fighting the ice pack for two weeks.

Their elation was premature, however.

Trouble came late in the evening. It was not dark for this was the time of the midnight sun.

The *Kite* hit a heavy floe and ground into the rotted ice as far as it could. Captain Pike, the master, signaled to reverse engines. The whaler started backward to get a running start for another assault on the ice floes.

As it went astern, broken cakes of ice, knocked loose by the *Kite's* last charge, hammered against the sides of the vessel. Suddenly a large one hit the ship's rudder. The jolt ran up through the wheel, but the quartermaster kept control.

The ship went on astern, the floe going with it. A few more yards and the floe jammed against a piled up mass of ice. The backward motion of the ship caused the rudder to be thrown completely over. The quartermaster was thrust aside and Peary was hit by the whirling wheel. He was smashed against the deck. Two bones in his leg were broken.

Dr. Cook reset the leg, but it was weeks before Peary could walk again. The crew advised him to return on the *Kite* to New York but he refused angrily and insisted on being carried ashore. They built him a hammock from which he could direct building of the camp, the small group moved on shore, and the *Kite* and its crew returned to New York.

The next months were a slow buildup for the great push to the top of Greenland. Walrus, seal, and bear meat had to be hunted and stocked for the push. Forward caches had to be established to store the food. Peary did not intend again to be stopped by hunger which he called the greatest danger of the Arctic.

After the long winter's preparations, Peary and one companion started the trek into the unknown. Dr. Cook went along for the first 130 miles, carrying extra supplies so that when he turned back, his stock would replenish those Peary and his companion had used, which meant that the final leg was started with full sleds.

It was a bitter journey, full of danger and narrow escapes from death, but at last, on July 4, 1892, Peary built a cairn of rock on the northernmost point of Greenland and left in it this note:

"Have this day, with one companion, Eivind Astrup, and eight dogs, reached this point via the Inland Ice from McCormick Bay. We have traveled over 500 miles. I name this bay 'Independence' in honor of that day, July 4th, dear to all Americans, on which we looked down into it."

(Twenty years later the cairn with the note was found by a later explorer.)

The next day he turned back, arriving at his base on August 6, after having been gone ninety-three days.

He had successfully demonstrated that Greenland was an island. He had also discovered the existence of ice-free land masses to the north of Greenland. He had determined the limits of the ice cap, and added many new names to the maps as he pushed the unknown back a little farther.

Peary's ambitions began to soar. Now he was dead set on the North Pole as his next goal.

When Peary, after two more expeditions to Greenland, announced his plans to find the North Pole, Richard Evelyn Byrd — who would follow him as America's greatest polar explorer — was ten years old and an avid reader of Commander Peary's heroic exploits in the North. In a few years his own career would start to parallel that of Robert Peary. Byrd, too, would join the Navy and finally branch out into polar exploration.

So many people had failed to reach the Pole that many now believed it impossible. Peary repeated his favorite motto: "If there isn't a way, I'll make one."

But it looked as if he had for once overreached himself and his ambition had carried him too far. Time after time he made a brave start, but troubles forced him back.

One of the greatest difficulties was the open leads. The North Pole — the geographical pole — is located over water. There is no land for hundreds of miles. The stresses and strains of the sea ice had piled up huge masses of ice, which added to the difficulty of travel. Sleds were broken. Dogs were exhausted and crippled. Men were tried to the breaking point. Storms were frequent. The constant movement of the water developed great cracks in the ice. These cracks, called "leads" by the explorers, sometimes stretched for miles. Sometimes they were small enough to jump over. Sometimes they were so large there was nothing to do but to wait impatiently for the ice to freeze again. Sometimes they were so great there was no choice except to turn around and struggle back to record another failure.

On one of the expeditions, bitter storms sapped the party's strength. With his food gone, his dogs dying, and his own toes frozen, Peary fell back to regroup.

It was in the dead of winter. The sun did not rise at all and moonlight proved insufficient to find a way back to the coast. But they blundered along and finally found their way. Peary started down the shoreline, seeking Fort Conger, a camp established fifteen years before by the ill-fated Greely expedition.

They went up the beach, hemmed in by cliffs impossible to climb. Before long their way was blocked. At some previous time the sea ice had broken. Huge slabs were hurled up on the beach, piling up until they jammed against the cliffs.

Although this seemed a barrier that would destroy them, Peary did not panic. He had faced death too often to give up just because everything seemed lost.

He kept searching along the ice dam and finally found a hole where the blocks had pyramided over each other. They were able to crawl through.

Later his frozen toes had to be amputated. He was left with just the little toe on each foot. Instead of getting easier because of his experience, Peary's Arctic travels were becoming more difficult. The physical pain, hunger and misery of this last trip exceeded all the others combined.

But all the difficulties made him more determined than ever to push on once more toward the North Pole.

So back he came in 1902 only to be stopped by broken ice. In 1905 Peary was again fighting cold, hunger and the shifting ice in still another desperate attempt to reach the top of the world.

This expedition was worse even than the one where his toes had been frozen. Caches or storages of supplies which had been laid down by supporting parties for him to pick up on the way back from the Pole were lost by the same storms which prevented him from reaching his goal.

The storms caused the ice pack to drift. The supply points were lost. At the same time the movement made leads which refused to freeze over.

Peary and his companion, Matt Henson, whom he had promised so long ago in Nicaragua to take to the North Pole, finally had to stop at 87°6' N. only 174 miles from the Pole — the farthest anyone had ever gone. The long march back was an epic fight against the savage ice and starvation.

The entire world was impressed by Peary's stubborn refusal to admit defeat. Other explorers paid tribute to his courage and persistence. Nansen, who had beaten him in being first to cross Greenland, said, "I don't know what I admire most about Peary — the energy with which he works year after year in spite of the most formidable odds or his never-failing readiness to overcome the greatest and the most unexpected difficulties."

The Navy now decided that their officer had wasted enough time fruitlessly charging the Pole. He was ordered back to duty. It was a cruel blow to his chances. He was now fifty years old, and for eighteen years he had striven towards his goal. Any delay now would mean the end of his Northern ambitions, for he would be too old to stand the rigors of the expeditions.

Fortunately he had friends who went directly to President Theodore Roosevelt, who ordered the Navy to put him on leave again — just as President McKinley had done a few years earlier. In gratitude, Peary named his new boat *Roosevelt,* and in 1908, at the age of fifty-two, he set out with loyal Matt Henson for what he knew must surely be his last attempt to raise the Stars and Stripes on the North Pole.

Once again he used the relay system. The other members went as far as they could and cached supplies for Peary's return. Then, 150 miles from the Pole the last one of them turned back, leaving Peary, Matt Henson, and four Eskimos for the final dash to the Pole.

On April 5, an observation of the sun showed them only three miles from their goal. The next day they made camp at the spot where his observations showed the goegraphical North Pole to be — at 90° North Latitude.

He was still afraid an equipment error might have thrown his calculations off. To offset this, he "boxed in" the Pole, traveling outwardly eight or ten miles to make doubly sure that he had truly reached the top of the world.

It was too early to celebrate, for they had the long difficult journey back. Worse yet, it was well into spring and the danger of leads cutting them off was greater than ever.

However, Nature — as if in apology for the past harshness toward the explorer — smiled for once. It was an easy trip back.

In his diary the happy explorer wrote: "The Pole at last. The prize of three centuries. My dream and goal for twenty years. Mine at last. I cannot bring myself to realize it. It seems so simple and commonplace."

It was well that he took pleasure in his remarkable achievement while he could. His great victory would turn to ashes in just a few days.

When the ship touched Labrador and was back in connection with civilization, Peary was stunned to hear that Dr. Frederick Cook was claiming that he had reached the Pole a year earlier, dog-sledding from an advanced base in Greenland.

This was the same Dr. Cook who had treated Peary's broken leg nineteen years before.

Eskimos told Peary that Cook's claim was untrue — that they were with him and the doctor had never left Greenland.

Peary wired his denial of Dr. Cook's claim and a great battle started between those who supported Cook and those who backed Peary's claim.

Peary was deeply hurt when General A. W. Greely, who led the ill-fated expedition of 1883 where two-thirds of the men died, sided with Cook against Peary. Peary had earlier written a criticism of the way Greely handled his expedition. Some naval officers, angry when plans were advanced to promote Peary over them, also spoke against the explorer.

Cook's proof was rejected by the only scientific body that saw it, but still his supporters fought Peary's claim. A bill was introduced in Congress to recognize Peary's claim and award him a gold medal. This was defeated.

Peary went to Europe where his claims were accepted and he was greatly honored wherever he went. He returned to the United States, and President Taft — the third American President to favor Peary against his enemies — put his support behind the explorer. He was given the "Thanks of Congress" and promoted to rear admiral in the Navy. Peary was then retired from the service.

In 1912 he became an ardent supporter of the newly

invented airplane and predicted that in a few years it would fly over the North Pole.

Among those impressed by this prediction was a young man who had long been thrilled by stories of Peary's heroic explorations in the Arctic. He was Midshipman Richard E. Byrd, who had just graduated from the Naval Academy at Annapolis.

As soon as he could qualify, Byrd became a naval aviator. Already he had his eye on becoming the first man to fly over the North Pole, doing in the air what Peary had done in a dog sled.

Thirteen years later, in 1925, Byrd was in command of the naval air units of the Navy-MacMillan Greenland expedition. MacMillan had been a member of Peary's last expedition.

The next year, just fourteen years after Peary's prediction, Byrd, with Floyd Bennett as co-pilot, made the prophecy come true when he flew over the North Pole.

He went on from there to heroic work in the Antarctic and like the man who inspired him, ended his career as a rear admiral despite many adversities.

Not only in their accomplishment, but even in their personalities, the two men were much alike. Both had a high regard for their men. Byrd never lost a man in his expeditions. Peary lost only one. Men who served with both praised their ability as leaders.

However, what is probably even more remarkable than their courage, was the way both Peary and Byrd withstood criticism leveled against them. That is the real mark of character.

The Hero of John F. Kennedy

Brother Joe

It was late in the afternoon of August 12, 1944 when Lieutenant Joseph P. Kennedy, Jr., looked out the side window of a Navy PB4Y Liberator bomber.

A Navy airman, holding a fire extinguisher beside one of the outboard engines, signaled that the propellers were clear. Kennedy hit his starter switches. The four-bladed propeller started to turn, there was a cough of fire from the exhaust, and the engine roared into life.

The watching airman with the extinguisher moved over where he could stand guard over the next engine. After all

John F. Kennedy

Joseph P. Kennedy, Jr.

were started, Kennedy slowly taxied to the end of the landing strip. He set his brakes so the big plane would not roll and pushed the throttles forward to rev up the engines. Swiftly and expertly he and his co-pilot, Lieutenant Wilford J. Wiley, went through their cockpit check to make sure everything was in perfect working order.

Occasionally on one of their previous twenty-eight bombing missions against the German targets they had ignored some deficiency rather than be left behind.

But this mission was different. Everything had to be perfect. No chances could be taken. The flight was too important. And nothing like it had ever been tried before.

Both men were acutely aware that this time they were not flying a bomber. They were riding a flying bomb!

On the other flights their job had been to drop bombs on the enemy target and get back home. This time they were not going to drop a bomb. They were going to drop the entire airplane!

Their target was the single most important one in the war at that time. Grim-faced planners, deep in bombproof dugouts, had decided that it would be impossible to get regular bombers through to blow up this target.

But they thought that one plane might do it if false attacks were launched on nearby targets at the same time. With the German defenses thus sidetracked, there was a chance that Kennedy and Wiley could get through — aim their plane at the target and jump out.

Behind them two other U.S. Navy planes would fly the bomber by radio control after its pilots left. Packed in the bomb bays and in the waist of the plane were 22,000 pounds of explosives.

The important target was the German V-2 rocket base. No V-2's had yet been fired, but spy reports about it had chilled the Allied command.

They had already seen what terrible damage the V-1 buzz bombs could do. More than 8,000 of these pilotless flying bombs were fired at London. They could only travel 360 miles per hour, and the fast Allied fighter planes managed to shoot down half of them. But even so, those that got through the fighter net knocked down more than 75,000 buildings, killing nearly 6,000 people and injuring 17,000 more.

Now, in August 1944, after nearly a year of terror from the flying bombs, Allied spies reported that the improved V-2 would weigh 14 tons and travel more than 3,000 miles per hour. No plane in the Allied forces could approach this terrific speed. It seemed that the enemy had come up with a perfect weapon — one for which there was no defense.

Fleets of bombers had been unsuccessful in knocking out production. Intelligence reports indicated that the new V-2's were being built in underground factories sunk deep in the heart of German mountains. The reports claimed that Hitler was stockpiling thousands of them in preparation for an aerial assault on London. It was hoped that this would bring the war to an end.

It was to destroy one of the new V-2 launching fields that Lt. Joseph P. Kennedy, Jr., took off on August 12, 1944. His Liberator bomber was packed with 22,000 pounds of TNT.

The flight was an experiment. If the flying bomb idea worked, then other planes would be sent over for the same mission.

Neither Kennedy nor Wiley had been told about this when they volunteered. All that either man knew was that there was a top secret project under way and that it had the code name "Project Anvil."

This was enough for Kennedy. If there were something unusual coming up, he characteristically wanted to be a part of it.

When he put his name on the volunteer list, he was jokingly reminded that he had only two more missions before he completed his assigned number of combat flights.

"Then you know what happens," a friend told him, meaning that Kennedy could return home.

"Sure I know what happens," Joe joked back. "After your thirtieth mission you fly your thirty-first!"

The other man shook his head. "You just don't believe they'll send you home, do you?"

Joe grinned. It was a happy-go-lucky smile — one of the things about him that people still remember.

"Who wants to go home?" he asked. "There are no Germans to fight back there."

Once the crew was selected things moved swiftly. Kennedy and Wiley needed little practice. After twenty-nine missions over Germany there was little anyone could tell them about aerial combat. They went to briefings to learn about their air route. Intelligence officers told them where to expect enemy air and anti-aircraft opposition.

They conferred with ordnance people, who placed the

high explosives in the plane, and received instructions on how to set fire to the fuses at the proper time.

The crews of the radio "mother" planes had been trained in the States before coming overseas. For months they had practiced taking over control of a Liberator by radio and guiding it to a target.

The controls were in a black box set in the cockpit between the pilot and co-pilot positions. In answer to radio commands, gears ground to move the planes controls.

Just before take-off, radio specialists slipped in preset tuning units to be sure the radio sending and receiving sets operated on frequencies which their air monitoring showed the Germans were not using. They were taking no chances on the airlanes getting jammed. Too much depended on the success of this mission.

The target was in Normandy. The three planes, the flying bomb, and its two radio controllers took off in the late afternoon for a strike timed slightly after darkness fell.

The lift off was smooth and tense watchers on the ground saw the planes disappear into the murky English sky. They headed directly across the English Channel. They were scheduled to set their fuses and bail out when they got to the French coast line. They would land in the Channel and be picked up by fast PT boats.

As the coast line appeared one of the pilots went into the back of the plane to set the fuses. The time was 6:20 P.M.

In the two Vega Ventura mother planes tense watchers waited for the signal to take over control by radio.

Suddenly there was a burst of flame in the darkening sky. A second explosion seemed to follow a second later. The

Liberator exploded. The middle of the plane vanished in boiling flame. Wings, nose, and tail section flew off and plunged toward the sea.

The horrified watchers in the mother planes circled, seeking a glimpse of opening parachutes. There was none.

They kept circling until they were absolutely sure there were no survivors. Then they headed back to England with the sad news that something unexpected had happened.

What did happen? No one knows. It was suggested that a gas leak might have filled the plane with explosive fumes which were set off by the fuses of the TNT. There was another suggestion, but never any proof, that German spies had learned of the mission despite its top secrecy and somehow had sabotaged the plane.

Back in the United States, word of Lt. Joseph P. Kennedy's death was taken very hard by another hero of the war, Lt. John F. Kennedy, who was to become President of the United States sixteen years later. John Kennedy grieved both for a brother and a personal hero.

Many men have tried to follow in the footsteps of their boyhood heroes. John F. Kennedy was not one of these. His hero died too young to leave footprints for his younger brother to step into.

What Jack Kennedy did was to continue Joe's footprints, walking surely toward the goal Joseph P. Kennedy, Jr. had set for himself — the White House.

In later life, Jack Kennedy made no secret of it. Joe had been his boyhood idol. He was the one all the other Kennedy boys looked up to. Joe was the strongest, the wisest, the gayest, and the best-liked. Whatever the rest

could do he could do better. He was the one who taught
them to play ball and to sail their boats in the harbor.

But it wasn't all blind hero worship by any means. One
of the things that Pat Kennedy taught his own son Pat back
in 1850 was "that second best is defeat." Pat, Jr., in turn
taught the same lesson to his son, Joseph Patrick, Sr., who
passed it along to Joseph Patrick, Jr.

Joe, Jr., taught it to Jack, Bobby and Ted. "Second best is
defeat." And that was true even if the one who beat you
was your own older brother.

All during his childhood John F. Kennedy struggled to
meet the goals set by Joe, Jr., and he never quite made it.

Sometimes the rivalry exploded into quarrels and fights.
Joe, Sr., was often away from home on business, and the job
of being an "assistant father" fell to Joe, Jr. Sometimes Jack
would resent his elder brother's bossiness and the fists would
fly.

Even after they left home the rivalry continued with Jack
vainly trying to match the records set by Joe in academic
work and in sports.

When the war came, Joe was the first to go. Jack followed
soon after. Now for the first time he seemed to forge ahead
of Joe. This was when his PT boat was sliced in two by a
Japanese destroyer in the Coral Sea. Jack, drawing on that
never-die spirit which Joe had taught him, saved his own
and the life of a comrade by towing the wounded man by a
strap held in his teeth.

It was a thrilling story of heroism and for once Jack was
ahead in the long race to beat his brother Joe.

Then one year later, Joe evened the scales when he

volunteered for Project Anvil. For this he was awarded the
Navy Cross after his death, second only to the Medal of
Honor.

The citation read: "Well knowing the extreme danger
involved and totally unconcerned with his own safety,
Lieutenant Kennedy unhesitatingly volunteered to conduct
an exceptionally hazardous and special operational mission.

"Intrepid and daring in his tactics and with unwavering
confidence in the vital importance of his task, he willingly
risked his life in the supreme measure of service."

After Joe's death, Joseph, Sr., had a talk with Jack. He
told him that it was his duty to take Joe's place as the
politician of the family.

But first Jack put together a book in memory of his
beloved brother. It was filled with reports from friends and
relatives about Joe. Jack himself wrote, "Joe did many things
well, as his record illustrates, but I have always felt that
Joe achieved his greatest success as an older brother."

Jack Kennedy had never dreamed of going into politics
himself. That had been Joe's field. The eldest Kennedy boy
never made a secret of his ambition. He was going to be
President and didn't care who knew it.

Professor Harold Laski of the London (England) School
of Economics remembered Joseph Kennedy, Jr., well.

"Joe," he said, "was interested in everything. He had a
great enthusiasm. What he liked, he liked with all his heart.
He had a great interest in politics and had his heart set on a
political career. He often sat in my study and submitted,
with that smile that was pure magic, to relentless teasing
about his determination, expressed many times, to be
nothing less than President of the United States."

The desire to be a politician was part of Joe Kennedy's inheritance. It began in 1847 when Patrick Kennedy came to the United States from Ireland to escape the starvation that followed the potato famine. The Irish in America were a minority and had to stick together politically to get along. Pat's son Patrick started a store and soon became a successful politician.

His work brought him in contact with another Irish politician whom he did not like particularly, but had to work with. This man was "Honey Fitz" Fitzgerald.

Neither man was happy when Pat's son Joseph fell in love with Fitzgerald's daughter Rose. But neither man interfered, and the couple were married.

So it was that Joe, Jr., was born into a household where the talk centered about politics. At an age when most boys were reading Tom Swift, Joe, Jr., was absorbed in "Honey Fitz's" tales of knock-down-and-drag-out political battles.

Later, Joe, Sr., would encourage his boys to discuss and debate the political issues of the day.

With such a background, it is no wonder then that young Joe wanted a political career — and being a Kennedy who had been taught all his life that "second best is defeat," he aimed for the top.

This was the seemingly impossible goal that Jack Kennedy took over from his dead brother and hero.

And in sixteen years Kennedy followed that dream of Joe's to the House of Representatives, the Senate, and then into the White House itself, making his hero's dream come true.

The Hero of Harry Houdini

The King of Magic

A MAN HUNG IN THE SKY. A rope twisted about his ankles was suspended from a beam between two skyscrapers. A straitjacket such as is used to restrain disturbed people in sanitariums was wrapped around his arms. Chains with huge padlocks encircled the jacket.

Far below amazed crowds watched the chained man struggle head down to free himself from his locks and chains. These had been carefully inspected earlier to see that no trickery had been employed.

Somehow — for he never revealed all his secrets — Harry

Harry Houdini

Robert-Houdin

Houdini, the Escape King, freed himself, climbed back up the rope and waved to the crowd below.

Another time they stripped the clothes from Houdini's body. Police searched him thoroughly to make sure he had nothing concealed anywhere. Then they put him in the strongest cell in the jail. To make things more difficult for this brash man who claimed he could escape from any jail, they handcuffed his legs and wrists to the iron bars of the cell.

Somehow, Harry Houdini got out of the handcuffs, opened the jail door and walked out.

Again, he cut a hole in the river ice one bitter winter. He had himself handcuffed, put in a box which was wrapped with chains and locked, and then had the box dropped through the ice into the dark river.

Somehow, Harry Houdini got out of this death trap and swam to the hole and climbed out, once again proving himself the Escape King and a master of magic.

It is no wonder that this incredible showman became Buffalo Bill's greatest rival as the number one hero of American youth.

As for Harry Houdini — he had been inspired by a man he considered tops in the world of magic. This remarkable man was Jean Eugène Robert Houdin, the greatest magician of all time and a man who had used his magic to stop a war!

When Harry Houdini first read about Robert Houdin he was completely fascinated. "My interest in magic and my enthusiasm for Robert Houdin came into existence together. He became my guide and hero," Houdini wrote later.

"When it became necessary for me to take a stage name, I added an "i" to Houdin's name for a friend told me that in the French language this would mean 'like Houdin.' I asked nothing more of life than to become in my profession like Robert Houdin."

Who was Robert Houdin? Today he is remembered only by students of the history of magic, but 110 years ago he was the master of magic.

In one of the most amazing feats of legerdemain he handed a loaded revolver to a man who hated him viciously.

"Aim at my heart and pull the trigger," he told the man.

The man, a French-hating Arab, cried: "I will kill you with pleasure, you French dog!"

He pulled the trigger. The flintlock pistol showered sparks into the flashpan. The exploding powder hurled a lead ball from the gun's barrel.

Robert Houdin faced the open muzzle of the gun, his heart beating wildly and with a silent prayer that his magic would save him—and in saving him, would stop a war.

Oddly enough, Robert Houdin's greatest magical performance was done at the request of the French government in an attempt to stop the fighting between the Arabs and French in Algeria.

And even more odd is the fact that it did!

Jean Eugène Robert Houdin was a clockmaker in Blois, France. One day he went to a book store to buy a book about his work. It was dark in the shop for the owner did not believe in wasting money on more than a single candle.

When Houdin asked for the clockmaker's manual, the

old man made a mistake and took down the book next to it. Neither he nor the young clockmaker noticed the error. When Jean Eugène got home, he was startled to see that he had purchased a book on how to perform magic tricks.

It was a wonderful book and made him dream of becoming a magician himself. It was not, however, a good book for a beginner and the boy did not learn very much from it.

Then one day he became deathly sick from eating contaminated food. In desperation he decided to go home. He climbed on a stagecoach in Tours for the journey back to Blois, but was so ill that he fell out during one of the turns.

He struck the ground in the dark, but the driver did not see him, and the coach rolled on in the night leaving Jean Eugène unconscious by the side of the road.

When he came to himself he was in the back of a traveling magician's wagon. The man, who called himself the Great Torrini, had found the unconscious boy and picked him up. He nursed Houdin back to health and for a year they traveled together, the older man teaching the boy all his tricks.

There was one trick he would never teach Jean Eugène Each time it was mentioned Torrini would cry bitterly. One day he told Jean Eugène why it made him so unhappy.

Years before Torrini had been a famous magician. His greatest trick was to take a loaded gun and fire it at his son's head. The audience could see the gun fire and smoke belch from its barrel, but instead of falling, Torrini's son caught the bullet in his teeth.

Before the act, the father would have someone in the

audience mark an X upon the bullet. He would then load it into the gun in full view of everyone.

The same person would be invited to inspect the bullet held between the younger Torrini's teeth. He would find it had the same X he had marked on it, proving it had indeed been fired from the flintlock pistol.

The act was a great success until one day something went wrong. Torrini pointed the gun at his son's head as usual. He pulled the trigger. The cock fell and the flint scraped across the steel. Showers of sparks fell into the flashpan. The gun roared. But instead of a smiling boy holding a bullet in his teeth, the horrified magician saw his son fall dead.

Somewhere the trick had gone wrong.

After he got out of prison, Torrini changed his name and left Italy. Although he had once performed in great theaters, he now went from village to village in a one-horse cart.

Robert Houdin learned how to do the pistol trick; but after he became famous himself, he did it only rarely. It was too difficult.

After a year the young man left Torrini and went back to clockmaking. He was very clever, and soon was making automata. These were amusing little figures operated by clockworks.

His masterpiece was a boy seated at a writing desk. When the clockwork was wound, the little figure could write answers to several questions. So cleverly were the gears arranged and connected with the concealed clock, that the little figure, when questioned, could write out the exact time of the day.

Houdin won a gold prize in the Paris Exposition with

his mechanized boy and it was bought by the famous P.T. Barnum for his circus in the United States.

In spite of his success, Robert Houdin finally gave up clockwork. He built himself a little theater in Paris and eventually became the most famous magician in the country.

His fame became so great that he was asked to give a performance before the king. The king's sister decided to embarrass the magician. She handed him a jewel box and asked him to tell her what was inside.

Robert Houdin had just been doing a mind-reading act with his son. The boy, Emile, was seated across the room with a blindfold over his eyes. When his father pointed to an object in the room, he would tell what it was.

The duchess suspected that the magician was using a secret code to tell his son what the objects were. Now she asked that Emile identify something that his father could not possibly see.

The great magician took the closed box in his hands. He looked at it with dismay. The duchess clapped her hands in glee. However, Robert Houdin's dismay was just window-dressing to make his royal audience think that he was in trouble.

"I have no idea what is in the box myself," he said slowly. "But I trust to the 'second sight' of my gifted son. Emile, my son, I know how difficult it is for you to see both through your blindfold and the top of this box. I know how it will exhaust you, but for this one time I beg you to try!"

With his speech, Robert Houdin was cleverly doing three things. He was making the trick seem harder to his audience. He was giving Emile a clue to drag the thing out. And third, he was telling him by a certain word inserted in the speech that it was a diamond pin in the closed box.

After a struggle, twisting and turning in his chair, Emile correctly identified the object as a diamond pin.

"A very clever guess, M. Robert Houdin," the king said.

The magician smiled. "Thank you, Your Majesty," he said, "it is true that my son might guess that it was a diamond pin in the closed box, but I doubt that he could possibly guess the *exact design* of that pin."

"No," said the king, who knew how the pin was shaped, "no one could possibly guess that."

"Then, Emile, my son, relate to His Majesty the design of the diamond pin hidden in this jewel case."

"It is in the shape of a peacock," Emile said.

Both the king and the duchess gasped. Robert Houdin smiled. "How many feathers are there in this gorgeous bird's tail?" he asked.

"Seven," said the boy, "and there are seven diamonds in each feather."

Robert Houdin turned and handed the box back to the duchess. She was so amazed that she presented the pin, worth several thousand dollars, to the magician's eleven-year-old boy.

It was long after the death of the king and the duchess that the great magician revealed the secret of the trick.

It was done with a "poison ring" which Torrini had given him many years before. These rings had once been fashionable in Italy for murdering one's rivals. The ring had a secret catch so the top could be swung back, revealing a tiny opening where poison was stored. It was a simple matter to wave one's hand over the victim's wineglass in the natural gesture one might use while talking. The poison would drop unseen into the glass. In the days of candlelight it could be done very effectively.

What Houdin did was to build a tiny mirror into what had been the poison compartment. Then, because of his skill as a watchmaker, he knew how to find the hidden spring that opened the jewel box.

Holding the box low, so it was obviously impossible for him to look into it, he gently opened it just barely enough so that by flipping back the top of the ring with his thumb, he could get a reflection in the mirror of what was in the box. It was done so quickly, while his royal audience was intent on what he was saying, that none detected the trick.

He had often used this trick in his theater to tell owners what initials were carved inside the closed covers of their watches.

Clever legerdemain such as this soon made Jean Eugène famous and when he decided to retire in 1850, he was credited with being the father of modern magic. Before his time magicians were not held in much esteem. He made magic an art.

Robert Houdin retired to his home in Blois and amused himself by making mechanical gadgets for his home. Then one day in 1856, a representative of the government came to him. He was asked to do his act again in an attempt to prevent war.

Robert Houdin was amazed. "But what can a magician do?" he asked. "I can wave a wand and make a rabbit appear from a hat. I can wave my hand and make a

handkerchief disappear, but, *monsieur,* I do not think any
man can wave a wand and make a war disappear!"

The government man smiled. "If any man can do so, M.
Robert Houdin, you are that man."

"I am flattered," the magician said, "but this is impossible."

"Please hear me out before you say that," the visitor said.
"You see we are not behaving as foolishly as you may think.
We are asking for magic to help us because it is magic
which is defeating us in Algeria!

"Let me explain. As you know, pirates operating from
Algeria did so much damage in the Mediterranean Sea
that France was forced to take over the country for the
protection of our shipping. Today a group of local priests,
called Marabouts, are trying to stir up another war against
us.

"These men are cheap magicians who go about doing
tricks to convince the people that they have miraculous
powers. They are becoming so strong that we expect the
war to break out at any time."

"I see, sir," the magician said slowly. "These false
prophets are using magic tricks to impress the superstitious
natives."

"That is correct," his visitor said. "One of the tricks which
makes a powerful impression on everyone is to prove that
the Marabouts cannot be killed."

"How is it done?" Robert Houdin asked, his face lighting
up with interest now that the subject was his beloved magic.

"The rascal loads a gun and gives it to someone to shoot
at him. But the magician says some strange words and the
gun refuses to fire. Then to prove there is nothing wrong

with the gun, the Marabout takes the gun and fires it into the ground. It is a most impressive exhibition. The natives have come to believe that he can protect them from French bullets the same way. We must expose these fake magicians or face a war in which thousands will be killed."

"I can see how it might do just that," the magician said thoughtfully.

"I know it is a trick," the French official said. "But for the life of me I cannot see how the rascal keeps that gun from firing."

"It is very simple, monsieur," Jean Eugène said. "I suspect he uses the old-fashioned gun. These weapons have a very small air hole in the side. The combustion chamber will not fire unless it has air. If this hole is stopped up, the gun will not fire. I think he puts a small plug in the hole when he loads the gun and then quietly removes it when he takes the gun back and fires it himself. It is an old trick of stage magicians."

"Excellent!" the official cried. "Then you will go to Algeria and expose this rascal?"

"I will do more than that," Robert Houdin said. "I will let him take a more modern gun which cannot be locked in this manner and shoot at me."

"But you will be killed!" the official cried.

Robert Houdin was silent for a moment thinking of what Torrini had told him about the trick, that it was too dangerous to use.

"No," he said at last. "I will not be killed if I am careful."

So Jean Eugène Robert Houdin went to Algeria to try

and wave his wand for peace. His first show was held in a mud-walled theater. He quickly ran through his tricks. There was an orange tree which bloomed and then put out fruit. This was followed by picking gold coins out of the air and giving them to the audience.

None of the tricks created any excitement. The theater was filled with native soldiers, high-ranking Arab chiefs, and Marabout priests whom the French officials wished to impress and frighten.

The magician's next trick created more of a stir when he took what appeared to be a small bottle and kept pouring coffee from it. The trick that followed shook the audience, and for the first time the audience began to show their superstitious fear.

Robert Houdin selected a strong man from the audience and asked if he was strong enough to lift a small box which the magician placed on a platform wheeled on stage.

Naturally the Arab lifted it easily.

"You are very strong," Houdin said. "But now I shall rob you of your strength by a simple wave of my wand!"

The Arab laughed and stooped to grab the handles of the box again. His big grin slowly faded as he struggled. The box would not budge. Bracing himself better, the huge Arab strained and heaved, but could not move the box he had lifted so easily a moment before.

Suddenly he stopped, and stared fearfully at the smiling magician. Then he gave a fearful yell and ran from the theater.

Now that the superstitious natives were uneasy, believing

in his magic power, Robert Houdin was ready to prove that
he was greater than their magicians in protecting himself
from fired bullets.

One of the Marabouts was selected to fire the gun. The
Frenchman watched the Arab check the vent hole to see
that it was open, and smiled.

"I will kill you!" the Marabout cried.

"Although you are a sorcerer, I am a greater one," the
Frenchman said in a loud voice so everyone in the theater
could hear him. "You will not kill me."

"We will see," the rebel Arab said confidently.

He selected one of the lead balls the magician held out
to him and made a mark on it. Robert Houdin took the
bullet and held it up so all in the audience could see. Then
he motioned for the Arab to pour powder into the gun
barrel. This was followed by wadding. Then the magician
dropped the lead ball into the barrel and put more wadding
on top. Finally a ramrod was used to pack the entire load
firmly into place.

The magician took his place fifteen paces away. The
eager Arab raised the gun and fired. The explosion rocked
the hall. The Arab gave a wild cry of triumph which turned
to stupefied surprise when the Frenchman did not fall.
Houdin smiled broadly so all could see the bullet firmly
caught between his teeth. When inspected it proved to
have the Marabout's mark on it!

The native was a magician himself. He knew, or thought
he knew, that he had been the victim of a clever trick. He
waited until the next day when French officials took
Houdin to a nearby village to do some tricks.

The Marabout met them in the market place. He bowed very low to the Frenchman.

"I now believe in your supernatural power," he said craftily.

"So?" Houdin asked, catching the wily look on the other man's face.

"Oh, yes," the Marabout said. "And since you are a *real* magician, you will be able to do your bullet trick here *in the open air!* See, I have brought a pistol for you to use!"

He held out a gun to the Frenchman. Robert Houdin was caught in a trap. The trick depended upon some clever sleight of hand. In a theater, under artificial light and separated from his audience by a stage, it was not too difficult. But out in the raw light of the sun with everyone packed so closely around him, he was not sure he could get away with the deception.

Worse yet, he had no fake bullets which he could switch for the real ones.

It was impossible to do the trick, but at the same time, if he backed down, he would lose all the respect he had built up.

Desperately Houdin sought some way to get out of the deadly demonstration without losing face.

"I must have a magic talisman to make me invulnerable," he said. "Unfortunately I left it in Algiers."

The Marabout laughed, thinking he had trapped Robert Houdin into admitting that he could not do the trick in the sunlight.

"I see you do not believe me," Houdin said quickly. "Very well, I can do without the talisman if I pray for six hours. It is now too late in the day to do the act for it will be night before I can finish my prayers. So I will let you fire your gun at me in the morning. Be here with your witnesses at eight o'clock!"

And so it was agreed, for prayer was something the devout Mohammedan natives could understand.

The next morning the famous magician kept his word and the trick went off perfectly. The Marabout was dazed. He could not believe what had happened. The natives fell on their knees in the sand and started to pray.

The native magicians were completely discredited and Robert Houdin received the thanks of the government for averting a war.

Years later the magician revealed how he had done the trick. It was in the book which so thrilled Harry Houdini and made him decide to become a magician himself.

This is what Jean Eugène Robert Houdin wrote:

"The trick, though so curious, is easily prepared. As soon as I was alone in my room, I took out my pistol case which had a bullet mold. I melted a piece of wax taken from one of the candles in my room. I mixed with it a little lampblack I had obtained by putting the blade of a knife over the candle. Then I ran this composition in the bullet mold."

He carefully experimented until he got just the right amount of black into the wax to make it exactly match the lead gray of a real bullet.

"Bullets thus prepared bear an extraordinary resemblance to lead," Robert Houdin wrote. "They are easily mistaken for that metal when seen from a short distance.

"After showing the lead ball to the spectators, I changed

it for my wax ball, and openly put the latter into the pistol."

This was a simple matter of palming the real bullet and holding up the wax fake to put in the gun barrel. The wax bullet was hollow and broke up when the wadding was pushed down by the ramrod.

"At the moment the pistol was fired, I opened my mouth to display the real bullet which I had placed there while everyone's attention was on the Marabout as he fired the shot."

The Hero of Jimmie Doolittle

The Early Eagle

THERE IS NO GREATER HERO of the air alive today than James H. Doolittle. His barnstorming and air races alone would insure him a permanent place in the roster of flying greats, but he went on from there to play an important part in civilian transport aviation. And he led the most daring flight of the war — the Doolittle Raid on Tokyo.

The carrier force which was supposed to carry Jimmie Doolittle's sixteen B-25 bombers within two hundred miles

Jimmie Doolittle

Louis Bleriot

of Tokyo were sighted by the enemy. Jimmie knew that if he took off farther out, the chances of any of the planes reaching Japan were very slight.

But he gave the command to go just the same. It was April 1942, and American morale was at a low ebb after the disaster of Pearl Harbor. The near-suicide raid on Tokyo was not expected to do much damage. It was intended to raise the spirits of the United States. Knowing this, Jimmie Doolittle chose to go even though it looked as if every man in the group might be killed.

This heroic flight served its purpose. It did raise American morale, and Jimmie Doolittle received the Congressional Medal of Honor and an imperishable record in the history of World War II.

After escaping death when his plane crashed in Japan, Doolittle went on to head the 12th and 8th Air Forces in the battle of Europe. He started the war as a major and ended as a lieutenant general.

When he became head of Space Technology Laboratories, he had a major role in the development of our nation's intercontinental ballistic missiles.

The examples set by the heroes of Jimmie Doolittle's youth made him the hard-fighting hero that he finally became.

As a schoolboy in Nome, Alaska, where his father sought unsuccessfully to find gold, the men he looked up to were the tough prize fighters who hammered each other with bare fists for the $25 that Tex Rickard paid them for each fight.

Although Doolittle was a short man, these fighters so

inspired him with their courage that he became a fighter himself and eventually won the bantamweight championship of California. Weighing only 105 pounds he knocked out men weighing 150 pounds.

As a prize fighter Jimmie Doolittle learned that of course courage and speed were essential — but that size, too, made little difference if a fighter really wanted to win. All of these qualities he carried with him into the war and they helped to make him a flyer-hero.

In 1908 Jimmie, like so many teen-agers of the period, got the flying bug. He loved mechanics and tinkering with machines, and was reading a magazine called *Popular Mechanics* when he ran across a story by Louis Blériot, who had just piloted an airplane of his own design in the most daring flight up to that time. He had crossed the English Channel from France to England.

The world was more thrilled by this feat than it had been by the Wright brothers' flight. Overnight aviation became respectable. Also, Blériot had made the world smaller by his historic flight.

As Doolittle, then fourteen, read Blériot's account of the flight, the world took on a new significance. He knew then that aviation would be the most important thing in his life. And someday he, too, would set world records like his new hero, the brave Frenchman, Louis Blériot.

The man who first inspired Jimmie Doolittle was then only thirty-six, but they had been eventful years. After leaving school, Louis started to develop his talent for mechanics and soon was hard at work on the problem of putting an engine on the glider.

His dream of building the first airplane was shattered when the Wright brothers in America built their Flyer in 1903. However, he was convinced that while the Wrights had been great pioneers, they were wrong in the way they went about the problem of making man fly.

To put his own ideas into effect he joined with the Voisin brothers in an airplane factory. During the first years he succeeded only in spending $150,000 while he survived fifty airplane crashes.

Finally, in 1908, he was sure that he had solved the problems that had nearly killed him so many times. He ended up with the world's first monoplane. He was sure that this single-wing plane would perform better than the Wrights' biplane which had two wings. He also put his engine out in front. In contrast to the Wrights' flying box kite, Blériot's graceful airplane looked almost modern.

He was so convinced that he had the better plane that he helped to dissuade the French government from buying a Wright Flyer.

His chance to prove what he could do came in July 1908. Lord Northcliffe, publisher of the London *Daily Mail*, put up a $5,000 prize for the first aviator to fly across the English Channel.

Blériot realized that winning this prize would make the world take his planes seriously. He immediately began to overhaul his monoplane for the flight.

But he was too late. Another French air enthusiast, Herbert Lathan, beat him to the punch. Lathan was a man completely without fear. Once, the engine dropped out of a plane he was flying. He crashed, crawled out of the wreckage, and started putting the pieces together again.

The wind was howling across the Channel the day Latham was to fly. He was advised that the weather was too bad. He shrugged off the advice and started anyway. Seven miles out to sea his motor sputtered and the plane started to fall.

A French Navy destroyer headed for the crash site. They found Latham calmly sitting on the floating wing. As soon as he got back to France he sent an order for another plane and set a new date for the flight.

Blériot's attempt wasn't much better. On a test hop, his machine caught fire and his leg was badly burned. Gas had flooded the carburetor and spilled over on the hot engine.

Even before his leg healed the dark-faced stern Frenchman was all set to try again. He had his plane stored in a shed at the top of a cliff overlooking the ocean near Calais, France.

When he went to bed the wind was high, but when he was roused at 4:30 the next morning, it had calmed somewhat. It was still too high for really safe flying, but like Latham, Blériot felt he couldn't wait. The new world of aviation was moving too fast. Word had already come from America that Orville Wright just five days before had flown to a world's record of one hour, 20 minutes and 43 seconds in demonstrating the Flyer to the U.S. Army at Ft. Meyer, Virginia.

He also knew that another American, Glenn H. Curtiss, was ready to try for a new record.

Aviation was growing so fast that anyone who hesitated

would be left behind in the race. Blériot refused to delay his flight and personally spun the propeller while his mechanic held down the tail to keep the little monoplane from spinning around in the gusty air.

From a teen-age balloonist, Blériot had graduated to gliders and then to airplanes. He had lived through fifty crashes. He knew very well that the risk he was now taking was greater than any of the others, but he was determined to go ahead.

There was a mist in the air and the aviator could see only a short distance ahead. A story often repeated says that he realized at the last moment that he had no idea where Dover, England, where he was supposed to land, might be. He leaned over and shouted to Monsieur Leblanc: "Where in the world is Dover?"

Leblanc pointed across the water and Blériot pointed the nose in that direction and waved for the men to release the plane.

In any event, this account is not included in the two stories published under the aviator's byline in *Popular Mechanics* in the United States and in the London *Daily Mail* in England.

In the *Mail* Blériot wrote: "Four thirty-five! All set! Leblanc gives the signal and in an instant I am in the air, my engine making 1,200 revolutions, almost its highest speed, in order that I may get quickly over the telegraph wires along the edge of the cliff."

The poles were difficult to see in the misty predawn. All the aviator could do was race his three-cylinder Anzani, 25 horsepower engine to its limits and trust to whatever luck he had not yet used up. He sailed over the wires with a few inches to spare and headed out to sea.

Fourteen-year-old Jimmie Doolittle read Blériot's story in *Popular Mechanics*. In imagination he soared into the mist with the gallant Frenchman in the little plane that weighed only two and a half times as much as its pilot.

"I have no apprehension, no sensations, not at all," Blériot wrote.

Below him the *Escopette,* a French destroyer, was steaming toward England. Its job was to keep Blériot in sight and pull him out of the Channel as another French ship had done for the last man rash enough to attempt to fly across the water.

Blériot waved as he went past the ship. He estimated her speed at about 26 miles an hour. His own was slightly above 40.

"Rapidly I overtake her," Blériot wrote, "traveling at a height of 250 feet. The moment is supreme. Below me is the sea, the surface disturbed by the wind."

A few minutes later he was enclosed in the mist. Doolittle thrilled as he read in *Popular Mechanics*: "I am amazed. There is nothing to be seen, neither torpedo destroyer, nor France nor England. I am alone. I can see nothing at all— not a thing!

"For ten minutes I am lost. It is a strange position to be alone, unguided, without compass, in the air over the middle of the channel."

In the London *Daily Mail*, Blériot gave a more detailed story. He told how he refused to alter the controls. He didn't know where he was going, but preferred to trust his airplane rather than himself. He kept flying. England was too big to miss. He might fail to make his scheduled landing point at Dover, but he was sure that he couldn't fail to find the big island.

Back in France there was less optimism. Word had been wirelessed from the *Escopette* that Blériot was lost.

As for Louis, he kept watching over the whirling propeller. After twenty minutes he saw the cliffs of Dover break through the mist. A castle was one of his landmarks. From it he knew that the wind had blown him far west of the spot where he was to land.

For the first time he began to doubt that he would make it to a landing. The great chalk cliffs were too high for him to fly over and the wind was getting worse. The tiny airplane began to toss in the turbulence.

"I press the lever," Louis told the *Mail*, "and turn easily to the west, reversing the direction in which I am traveling. Now indeed I am in difficulties, for the wind here by the cliffs is much stronger, and my speed is reduced as I fight it."

For a moment Louis considered turning back to France. He felt he had enough gasoline to get home and that might be safer than risking a landing in the unruly wind.

But a man who would risk his life on the impossible gamble of flying an airplane across the channel was not the kind of a man to take the easy way out.

Louis turned in a wide circle. "Again the wind blow. I see an opening in the cliff. I cannot resist the opportunity to make a landing."

Off to the side he could see a man waving a French

tricolor flag. It was a member of Blériot's ground team who had been sent to England to mark the landing field. Louis banked and headed for the spot.

"I attempt a landing; but the wind catches me and whirls me round two or three times."

It was clear that the frail craft did not have the power to buck the strong English winds and come down for a landing.

Blériot circled again, straining against his safety belt as the little plane tossed around. He was so close to doing something no man had ever done before and he did not intend to be cheated of success in his trans-Channel flight.

He knew from bitter experience gained in fifty wrecks, in both gliders and airplanes as well as free balloons, that once an engine stops and power fails, a plane will go down.

He came over the landing spot still another time. "At once I stop my motor. Instantly the machine falls straight upon the land from a height of 65 feet." The thin struts collapsed and his bicycle wheels buckled, but the frame held steady. Louis Blériot climbed out of his monoplane. In twenty minutes he had turned himself from a "nut" into an international hero. The short land hops aviators had made before aroused interest, but few took them seriously.

For the first time Blériot showed the world that the airplane had passed beyond the toy stage.

In the United States the Wright brothers were still demonstrating their Flyer to the Army. It was a better plane than Blériot's, and the Wrights were better aviators, but they were quiet, secretive men who shunned publicity. Blériot's flight, on the other hand, was the daring, spectacular

kind of stunt that captures the public's imagination. He
sold the world on aviation, and Doolittle was part of that
world.

A few months later Jimmy had another hero—a man
who had been in aviation as long as Blériot and for a time
was even more famous. He died young, however, while
Blériot went on to become a famous designer and builder
of the Spad, the famous fighter plane used by Eddie
Rickenbacker, the great American fighter ace of World
War I. Blériot lived to be seventy-four.

The man who next captured Jimmie Doolittle's imagination was a Brazilian daredevil. Like Jimmie, he was a very
small man who packed the courage of ten heroes in his
slight frame.

This man was Alberto Santos-Dumont. His father was a
millionaire coffee grower and Alberto looked frail and not
very manly.

His looks were deceptive for he had the soul of a lion. He
started out trying to race the new horseless carriages, but
quickly found this too tame. He took to the new sport of
gliding because it was more dangerous. Soon he left gliding
for the even more dangerous sport of flying in hydrogen
balloons.

Not satisfied with this, he attempted to rig up his
automobile engine to drive his balloon. Finally, in 1901, he
built a cigar-shaped dirigible 66 feet long and 11½ feet in
diameter. The bag was filled with highly explosive hydrogen.
Below it was a catwalk of light metal tubing. It was nearly
as long as the balloon bag.

All sorts of queer things happened. Each time a cloud

passed over the sun the gas pressure in the bag went down
and the bag sagged in the middle, letting the whole thing
drop to the ground. Another time he caught the corner of
the balloon on the edge of a building. It collapsed again.
When the fire department arrived, there was Alberto calmly
sitting in the ropes waiting for them to get him down. Five
times he landed in trees in the Bois de Boulogne Park in
Paris.

The mad Brazilian became the joke of the town, but he
didn't mind. He had a dream. And one day that dream
came true.

The astonished Parisians saw Alberto's flying ship sailing
around the Eiffel Tower. A large paddle of light bamboo
was at the back and the daring little balloonist was using it
to steer a turn around the tower.

As he turned, the airship lost altitude. The tail went down.
The breathless watchers below saw Alberto's slight figure —
he weighed only 110 pounds — racing along the catwalk to
the front of the balloon. His weight balanced the drop and
the dirigible was once more on an even keel.

Alberto raced back to the rear to resume steering. Then,
when there was another imbalance, he raced back to the
front again. This went on continually.

The airship had taken off from St. Cloud three miles
away in an attempt to win the $25,000 prize offered by the
Aero Club de France for the first person to fly a seven-mile
course in an airship in less than an hour.

Alberto circled the Eiffel Tower four times and then
pointed the nose of his airship back the way he came. All
the balancing and the up-and-down movements were con-

trolled by shifting his own weight along the catwalk. So it was that although Alberto Santos-Dumont was the first man to fly more than seven miles on a straight course in a controlled-flight balloon, he also *ran* just about every step of the way!

He landed back at his starting point in 20 minutes and 30 seconds to become the fastest man in the world!

At that moment Santos-Dumont stopped being "that madman" and became the great hero of the day. They cheered as he sailed down the streets of Paris *between* the buildings. They cheered when he crashed on top of a hotel but walked away uninjured. They cheered even louder when he took the prize money he won for the Eiffel Tower flight and gave it to the poor of Paris.

In 1902 he tried to fly across the Mediterranean Sea but crashed in the bay off Monte Carlo. The next year he came to America and thrilled the country with spectacular exhibition flights.

Although these flights made him world-famous, he had not yet aroused the enthusiasm of little Jimmie Doolittle. That was to come later.

Alberto soon grew tired of the unwieldy dirigible balloons and after the Wright brothers proved that a heavier-than-air machine could fly, he turned to aircraft experiments. Soon he was building his own planes.

He was completely unique as an aircraft inventor. He wanted nothing for himself except the sheer joy of flying. So he refused to patent his work. Everything he invented he gave freely to the world.

This is how Jimmie Doolittle first heard of him. Alberto designed a tiny one-man plane that was little bigger than a bicycle. It was powered by a tiny two-cylinder motor that sat on top of the mono-wing. The pilot sat between the two bicycle landing wheels and operated the controls with a wheel. He called it the "Demoiselle" and gave complete plans and blueprints to *Popular Mechanics*. The magazine sold them for $2 to all who missed their publication in the magazine.

Jimmie Doolittle had been working with gliders and his heart went out for a "Demoiselle." He reasoned that a motor-cycle motor would be sufficient to lift his weight instead of the two cylinder engine Santos-Dumont had used. He did not know then that the little Brazilian outweighed him by only five pounds.

He became a prize fighter to get enough money to buy a second hand motorcycle. Fortunately, for his glider was faulty and no doubt would have killed him if he could have gotten it into the air, a high wind wrecked it completely before he could make his first flight.

He had to give up flying to work in the Nevada mines, but a few years later, as a teen-ager, he volunteered for the Air Service when the United States entered World War I. here he really learned to fly and went on to become a famous racing pilot, winning air meet after air meet. He pioneered blind flying and the use of high octane fuel for airplanes. After that came his spectacular air raid on Tokyo and his splendid leadership of the 8th Air Force in England.

One can't help thinking that those grand old eagles of the early skies, Louis Blériot and Alberto Santos-Dumont, would be extremely proud of the boy they had inspired, who became an air hero himself.

The Hero of General U.S. Grant

Hero of Three Wars

WHEN CONGRESSMAN TOM HAMER appointed Jesse Grant's son Hiram to West Point, a disgusted neighbor said, "Why didn't Tom appoint somebody with sense enough to do the district credit?"

He was echoing everyone who knew Hiram Ulysses Grant. In all the history of famous generals, Hiram seemed the least likely to succeed as a soldier.

He disliked the army and army life. He hated to wear the uniform. He had little use for fighting. Furthermore it had not been his idea to be a soldier.

137

General U. S. Grant

General Winfield Scott

One day Jesse said to his son, "I think we can get you an appointment to West Point."

"But I won't go," the dismayed boy said.

"I think you will," the father said quietly.

And so Hiram went, hating every minute of it and determined to get out at the first chance.

Through a mixup he went not as Hiram U. Grant, but as Ulysses S. Grant. The appointing congressman got mixed up and put the wrong name on his papers and the military academy refused to change it.

It was hardly the congressman's fault. No one ever called the boy Hiram. Many called him Hug — from his initials. This humiliated the boy so much that he changed his name to Ulysses Hiram Grant. This did not help. The neighbors, seeing no good in him, changed Ulysses to "Useless."

This was the unlikely candidate for a military career who went to West Point in May, 1839 to take his entrance examination. He was surprised and disappointed when he was accepted.

As an old man he wrote, "A military life had no charms for me. I had not the faintest idea of staying in the Army even if I should be graduated, which I did not expect."

Strangely, although he hated Army life, the two people he admired most in life were both military men, representing the exact opposite of everything "Sam" Grant wanted in life.

We have no record of any heroes in Grant's early life. Seemingly he drifted through childhood without much interest in anything but horses. Then as a seventeen-year-old West Point Cadet he found someone to admire.

Let us have Grant tell us how he first saw his hero:

"During my first year General Scott reviewed the cadets. With his commanding figure, his quite colossal size and showy uniform, I thought him the finest specimen of manhood my eyes had ever beheld, and the most to be envied. . . . In fact, I regarded General Scott and Captain C. F. Smith, the Commandant of Cadets, as the two men most to be envied in the nation. I retained a high regard for both to the day of their death."

Captain Smith earned Grant's regard when he kept the young man from being thrown out of the military academy for breaking rules.

And Grant's admiration for Lieutenant General Winfield Scott grew as he served under the famous hero of the War of 1812. In 1846, during the Mexican War, Grant was ordered to take some men forward to test the enemy strength at San Cosme on the road to Mexico City. He ran into Mexican soldiers. Instead of retreating, Grant had a small cannon dismantled and carried piece by piece into the belfry of a church on the main road. From here he could shoot over obstructions straight down into the enemy camp. The Mexican troops broke and ran. Their confusion, the delighted General Scott said when he personally congratulated Grant, helped to win Mexico City for the U.S. Army and ended the war.

This was a proud moment for Captain "Sam" Grant, as he was called then. He was to feel the same pride years later when his old hero again complimented him. This was right after General Robert E. Lee surrendered to Grant at Appomattox to end the Civil War. The old soldier sent

Grant the first copy of his autobiography that came off the press. On the flyleaf Scott wrote: "From the country's oldest general to its greatest general."

Who was this man whom General Grant called "one anyone could envy?" Winfield Scott was the country's most famous soldier through all the periods of Grant's life—as a boy, young man, and middle aged man.

He was a Virginian, born in 1786. He grew up loving argument and politics. Since the law was the place he could get plenty of both, he read for the law and was admitted to the bar when he was twenty.

Although he never indicated any leaning towards a military career, we can detect it now in his choice of personal heroes. They were Julius Caesar and his fellow Roman, Scipio Africanus. Young Winfield never tired of reading Plutarch's accounts of their lives.

In 1807 Winfield Scott had gone to Richmond, Virginia, to attend the famous treason trial of Aaron Burr. The charge was a conspiracy by Burr to take over the Western side of the Mississippi and set up an independent government.

On June 22 news hit Richmond even more shocking than the trial. The fifty-gun British cruiser *Leopard* had stopped the United States frigate *Chesapeake* and searched it for British Navy deserters.

The United States vessel was not equipped for battle having only one gun in commission. Even so, the gallant crew tried to fight. The British ship fired three broadsides into the *Chesapeake*. The mainmast fell, dragging down a cloud of canvas sails and rigging. The ship's hull was leaking badly. Twenty-one American sailors were hurt. Two

Americans and one British navy deserter were carried off
to serve on the English ship.

It was the beginning of British seizure of American vessels
which would lead, five years later, to the War of 1812.

The country was in an uproar. President Jefferson, knowing that the nation was unprepared for war, tried to keep
the peace. He did forbid the British ships to come into
American waters but the captains arrogantly ignored the
order. Jefferson asked the governor of Virginia to use the
state militia to prevent the English from landing to
replenish their water supply.

The governor called for volunteers and among the first
to march was Winfield Scott—in a uniform that had its
seams opened in spots to make it big enough for his huge
form.

If Jefferson wanted to keep from getting into a shooting
war, he picked the wrong man in twenty-two-year-old
Winfield Scott. Scott's education had secured an immediate
promotion to Lance Corporal. One night he was sent on
patrol with a squad of men to watch for British landing
parties.

They found a ship's boat from the *Leopard,* the same ship
that had caused the trouble by firing on the *Chesapeake.*
The boat was commanded by a teen-age midshipman and
had been up the river to refill water casks.

Winfield ordered the British to stop. But the midshipman
urged his crew to hit their oars. Scott, shouting for his men
to follow, spurred his horse into the shallow stream to cut
off the boat's retreat.

He took his prisoners back to camp, but found that he

had embarrassed the President who wanted to avoid trouble. Orders came down from Washington to release the prisoners. "We applaud your vigilance," the President said, "but since we are not at war we cannot hold the prisoners."

Disgusted, Winfield Scott went back to riding the circuit as a country lawyer. But he missed the excitement and glory of military life.

Then, in 1808, sure that war was coming with England, Congress decided to add more officers to the Army. Scott contacted his political friends and they managed to get him an offer of a captaincy in the light artillery.

Winfield was so overjoyed that he did not wait to mail a letter accepting the commission. The mail would not go off until morning. Instead he rushed to the post house and found a stage leaving for Washington. He gave his acceptance letter to a passenger to carry for him.

The Army was a very rough place in those days. Almost everyone got into some kind of trouble. Winfield Scott was no exception. His pay was suspended for twelve months.

He had now grown to love the Army so much that he turned down the suggestions of friends that he resign. He would stick out his punishment.

But before the year had passed, he was demanding to have his pay restored. He used his legal knowledge and presented an argument that twelve months meant *lunar months*. This would be forty-eight weeks. If the court-martial had meant a *year*, it would have said a *year*.

The War Department, confused by this reasoning, restored Scott to full pay four weeks early.

Having learned that it is possible to win an argument

with the Army, Scott spent the rest of his life trying to win others. Sometimes he won. Sometimes he lost. But he never stopped trying.

Hotheads in the government were certain the U.S. Army could easily capture Canada so when war was finally declared, a force under General Van Rensselaer was sent to take the British possession. The big battle came at Queenston just across the Canadian border.

It was disastrous, but Scott emerged as a hero. When the American troops broke under the combined British-Indian assault, he jumped upon a log and made a fiery speech that sent them back into action. The battle was lost, because reinforcements refused to cross into Canada, claiming as militia they were not required to fight outside the United States. Winfield Scott was among the captured.

He was returned to the States in a prisoner exchange after endearing himself to the captured enlisted men by fighting the British over their treatment.

As a colonel, he returned seven months later when the attempt was made again to take Canada. This time the target was Fort George on the Niagara River just above the Falls.

In the wild battle that followed the British decided to evacuate the fort and the general gave orders to blow up the powder magazine. He was determined to destroy the fort so the Americans could not use it.

Winfield caught a horse left riderless when a British officer was shot and tried to get to the fort to put out the fuses. He galloped into the stockade in a desperate attempt to save the powder.

Before he could reach it, however, there was a terrible explosion. Dirt and shattered timber were hurled skyward and Scott was knocked off his horse. His collar bone was broken, but he refused to stop. Painfully he climbed back on the frightened horse and managed to get the animal under control as he galloped off in pursuit of the enemy.

Scott continued to perform heroically even though the American invaders suffered defeat after defeat in Canada. His reputation was so great that President Madison called him to Washington to ask his opinion on the conduct of the war. Soon after, when he was only twenty-seven, he was made a brigadier general. He was the youngest general in the Army.

Even greater glory came to Scott in the Battle of Chippewa. He led the First Brigade. Blue cloth for uniforms was not available and they went into battle wearing gray — the only cloth the military tailors had.

It was a tremendous victory — the first great victory of the Army in the war. Again Scott was hailed as a hero. The next year (1815) Congress ordered that West Point cadets would now wear gray uniforms to honor the "gray line" that Winfield Scott had led to victory at Chippewa.

He ended the War of 1812 as a major general. The next year found him involved in the Black Hawk War, in which Abraham Lincoln fought as a captain. Scott warred against the Seminole Indians in Florida. And he fought with many of the Presidents he served. He served a total of thirteen Presidents from Jefferson to Lincoln.

When the Mexican War began in 1846 it seemed for a

while that he would be left out of it. He had outraged
President Polk by claiming the war was unnecessary.

General Zachary Taylor was put in charge of the American
forces until the campaign slowed down. Then Polk called
Winfield Scott in. He did not remove Taylor, but sent Scott
to start another push.

Scott landed his forces at Veracruz, swept on through
Cerro Gordo and on to Mexico City in a brilliant campaign.
His chief of staff was Colonel Robert E. Lee. Both Colonel
Lee and Captain "Sam" Grant noticed each other, but
neither dreamed that in fourteen years they would be on
opposite sides in the most terrible war in our history.

After the war Scott continued to serve as general in chief
of the Army, too powerful and too well liked by the people,
for either President Polk or President Taylor to remove
him—although he was disliked by both.

The next President, Fillmore, was his friend, but Scott
ran for the presidency himself and was beaten by James
Pierce. Pierce appointed Jefferson Davis as Secretary of
War. Davis hated Scott, but could not remove the famous
old general. For the next few years the two fiery men
fought each other bitterly.

General Scott clearly saw the coming Civil War and
tried to strengthen Federal forts in the South. He was
balked at every turn and when the war came the North
was unprepared.

Remembering his old chief of staff, Scott wanted to give
command of the Northern field armies to Robert E. Lee for
Scott was now too old to lead in combat. Due to his bad

health he could no longer even ride a horse. Lee refused, preferring to serve his state rather than his nation.

So many Southerners were leaving to join the rebel forces that the new President, Abraham Lincoln, wondered about the loyalty of his Virginia-born general-in-chief.

Once again the old warrior had to battle — this time for his reputation.

While he was trying to convince President Lincoln of his loyalty, friends brought him an offer to join the Confederacy. Scott was outraged.

"I have served my country, under the flag of the Union, for more than fifty years!" he cried. "And as long as God permits me to live, I will defend that flag with my sword, even if my own native state assails it!"

In the South an angry newspaper cried, "He has become a Yankee! What a lasting disgrace."

Lincoln was satisfied, but Scott's enemies kept working against him. He was blamed for the Army's unpreparedness. Worse, General George McClellan kept insisting that Scott was too old and interfered with the plans of younger and better men. Finally things got so bad that Scott was retired and McClellan appointed general in chief.

McClellan failed miserably to stop the Southern armies, and Lincoln honored Scott by making a secret trip to ask the old soldier's advice about a successor to McClellan.

In the meantime General Grant was confounding everyone by winning battles when other Union generals were failing. Grant had quit the Army after serving under Scott in Mexico, but returned at the outbreak of the Civil War.

He climbed in rank as quickly as Scott had done in the War of 1812.

Enemies tried to discredit Grant to Lincoln. The President waved them away. "I can't spare him," he said. "He *fights!*"

Too old now to return to command, Scott spent his time writing his life story, sending the first copy to General Grant.

When Grant came to New York after the war ended, his first stop was to pay respects to the old soldier he had admired so long.

The following year, New York merchants, knowing how much Grant admired Scott, had the old general's portrait painted as a gift to Grant. They asked Scott to make the presentation.

But Scott was too ill. He died at West Point not long afterward in May, 1865.

The Hero of Mickey Mantle

The Man Who Struck Out

His name was "Mutt" Mantle and he lived only for baseball. His father had been a pitcher on a semi-professional ball club and Mutt had dreamed that he might toe the mound himself someday.

But as a baseball player, Mutt struck out. Like so many boys who dream of becoming famous, Mutt did not quite have what it takes to make the big time.

This did not lessen his love for the game. Baseball was the one great interest in his life. He thought about it, dreamed of it, and never got over the idea that he had

Mickey Mantle

E. C. Mantle

struck out as a player because he had not been trained early enough.

"Someday," he vowed, "I'm going to have a son. I'm going to give him a baseball the day he is born."

"That's a mite early, El," his father said. He never called Elvin Mantle "Mutt" as the others did.

"No, Dad," Mutt said. "You can't start training to be a ballplayer too early. Mickey is going to be a big league ballplayer. I know he is because you and I are going to make him one! You just wait and see!"

The older man smiled at his son's enthusiasm. "Your grandmother used to say: 'Don't count your chickens before they hatch.' A lot of families never have any sons at all. Did you ever stop to think that your 'Mickey' might turn out to be a 'Mabel'?"

"Nothing doing," Mutt said firmly. "I'm settling for nothing but a son. And he's going to settle for nothing but a catcher's place on the New York Yankees ball club!"

"But *if* Mickey should be a Mabel—?" his father said jokingly.

"Then the New York Yankees might as well get used to the idea of having a lady catcher!" Mutt retorted. "We're going to have a big leaguer in this family, Dad!"

And he was right. The man who never had a chance in baseball himself lived to see his son a member of the New York Yankees.

But he was wrong about his being a catcher for the young man became one of the greatest hitters in the history of the game and his name will be remembered as long as baseball is enjoyed.

When little Mickey was born in October 1931, there was some talk among his relatives that he should be named Charles since both his grandfathers had that name. Mutt didn't like to hurt anyone, but he was firmly opposed to this idea. His big-league baby was going to be named Mickey after Mickey Cochrane, the great catcher for the Philadelphia Athletics ball club.

"But Cochrane isn't doing so well this year," Mutt was told.

Mutt shook his head. "I'm not turning my back on a friend just because he's had a bad year."

The others smiled, but not his wife. She knew how much her husband loved baseball and how Mickey Cochrane had become his special hero. Cochrane was just the kind of man and player that Mutt had dreamed of being himself. Although Mutt had never met his hero, he had talked about and followed Cochrane's games so fervently that he felt and spoke of him as "my friend."

"Well," Mrs. Mantle said, "why don't we compromise by calling him Mickey Charles?"

Mutt Mantle had not been joking when he said his son was going to be a big-league ballplayer. It was even less of a joke when he said he was going to give him a baseball the day he was born. The future Yankee was only a few hours old when Mutt placed a baseball in the baby's crib.

Mutt knew that he would have to learn patience — for it would take many, many years to build Mickey into a ballplayer. But he began almost at once. At six months the future big-leaguer had a baseball cap. At eighteen months he was doing a good job of rolling a ball back to his father.

At two he had a bat but he wasn't big enough to swing it. At three he was taught to count. But Mutt's mathematical teaching stopped after the boy learned to count nine innings The rest his mother would have to teach him.

At five, he was belting a tennis ball across the yard. At six, Mutt and Grandpa started teaching him switch-hitting, hitting first from the right and then the left side of the base.

Mutt quit his job in the lead mines near their home in Oklahoma and bought a farm so there would be more room to play baseball. He also thought the hard, outdoor work would help build the strong body a big-leaguer needed.

But this was Oklahoma in the years of the Dust Bowl. There was no rain. Crops died. Blowing sand piled up on the barren land. Farmers were starving.

Reluctantly, Mutt went back to the mines. He had struck out once again. But there was plenty to ease his disappointment. Mickey was coming along as a ballplayer and father and son were inseparable. Most fathers find some time to play with their sons, but Mutt went far beyond fatherly pride and devotion. He was never too tired, no matter how hard he had worked that day in the mines, to throw a few balls for Mickey's batting practice. He was never too busy to tell the boy about the great games of the past and the great players who had played them.

Grandpa Mantle was in the act too. The three of them made up a team that confidently believed it was heading for the Yankee Stadium.

Once Mutt drove several hundred miles from Commerce, Oklahoma to St. Louis, Missouri so Mickey could see his first big-league game.

At eleven Mickey was playing on a team with boys in their teens — and outplaying them all. Now Mutt and Grandpa knew for sure that their years of work had not been wasted. Mickey was a ballplayer.

And so it went — the slow climb from sandlot to Class D baseball clubs and finally that glorious day when he first put on a Yankee uniform.

He thought he had it made then. Both Joe DiMaggio, the greatest ballplayer of his day, and Casey Stengel, the great Yankee manager, told him he was great.

But something happened. Mickey was too tight. He tried too hard. Somehow his bat, which had had no trouble connecting with the ball before, now fanned the breeze.

After he piled up fifty-two strike-outs, Casey Stengel had enough. Mickey turned in his big-league uniform and was sent down to the minor-league club at Kansas City.

He was told that if he could learn to hit again, the Yankees would take him back.

It was a grim, determined nineteen-year-old ballplayer who toed the sack at home plate in his first game with Kansas City. He had to make good not only for himself, but for Mutt Mantle as well.

He struck out.

The next game was the same.

Things got worse instead of better. For ten straight games he never got a single hit.

He knew he was through — washed out — a failure at nineteen years old.

That was when Mutt took a few days off from the mine and came down to Kansas City to see the baseball player he had prodded along since he was a child.

"How are you doing, son?" Mutt asked in his Oklahoma drawl.

"No good at all, Dad," the miserable ballplayer replied. "I'm just not good enough to play in the major league. I might just as well quit right now and go home with you."

Mutt didn't say anything. Mickey waited for his dad's sympathy. All through his life when things got tough, he could count on Mutt to cheer him up.

But this time he got a surprise.

Mutt looked at him sort of sadly. "If that's the way you feel," he said quietly. "I guess you had better come back to Oklahoma with me. I can get you a job in the mines again. You can crawl back in the hole and stay there."

Mickey was surprised and ashamed of being a quitter. He shoved the idea of going back to Oklahoma out of his mind. The rest of the evening he and Mutt talked of baseball and baseball players just as they used to when Mickey was growing up.

The next day the slump was broken. Mickey Mantle slammed out ten home runs in a row. The Yankees, who had discarded him in July, sent him a call in late August to come back. He went back and this time he stayed to become one of the greatest ballplayers of all time.

And he knew he owed it all to his father, but he didn't know then *just* how much he owed to the quiet Oklahoma miner who struggled for nineteen years to give his son the chance he had wanted but never got himself.

Mutt Mantle was fatally ill the day he went down to Kansas City to bolster his son's sagging spirits. He was dying of leukemia.

Always before he had sympathized with Mickey, but now he sensed that Mickey had to make his own decision. Wisely, he let his son know that he thought he was a quitter. Stung into action Mickey went back and made the grade.

Then, just as it seemed that fortune was smiling, Mickey tore some muscles in his leg. It was extremely painful, but what hurt even more was the terrible fear that he would never play baseball again. All during the winter Mutt kept after Mickey to see that the injured leg was properly exercised.

"When the time comes, you'll be in there," he told his son.

"I know it, Dad," Mickey replied grimly. "You've shown me the way. Nothing's going to stop me now."

And nothing did. He got three solid base hits in his first game.

This triumph was followed by a bad jolt. Mutt Mantle died. Mutt had known that he was going, but he had kept it from his son. He didn't want any worry about himself to hurt Mickey's chances for a comeback. So he went off alone to a hospital in Colorado knowing they could not help him. The doctors had told him that nothing could be done and he did not want his family to see him slowly dying. Bravely, Mutt faced the end alone.

Not long before he died he said his dreams for Mickey had been realized. He had seen his son make the big league and had seen him play in the World Series. "Now," he added, "I don't care if I strike out myself. I've seen everything I ever wanted to see when my son belted that ball over the fence in the Series."